origami
1-2-3

origami
1-2-3

David Petty

Sterling Publishing Co., Inc.
New York

© D&S Books

Library of Congress Cataloging-in-Publication Data Available

10   9   8   7   6   5   4   3   2   1

Published in 2001 by Sterling Publishing Company, Inc.
387 Park Avenue South, New York, N.Y. 10016

First published in the U.K. by D&S Books
Cottage Meadow, Bocombe, Parkham, Bideford, EX39 5PH

Distributed in Canada by Sterling Publishing
c/o Canadian Manda Group, One Atlantic Avenue, Suite 105
Toronto, Ontario, Canada M6K 3E7

Editorial director: Sarah King
Editor: Judith Millidge
Project editor: Clare Haworth-Maden
Designer: Axis Design
Photography: Colin Bowling

Sterling ISBN 0-8069-7573-3

contents

introduction

Origami in the West

In common with the origins of origami in the East, the origins of origami in the West are shrouded in the mists of time. Mere fragments of information are all that we have to build on. What can be said is the there was an early tradition of folding cloth in the form of clothing and napkins. In the 16th century, for instance, there are records of elaborate napkin-folding. Papyrus, the first form of paper in the West, was apparently foldable, as there is one example in Milan of an Egyptian folded map. Its preservation seems miraculous, but less important forms of paperwork have not survived.

During the 4th century, the popes were usually attended by ceremonial fans, or "flabelli," some of which were made from folded parchment.

Paper-folding had to wait until the secret of papermaking was passed on to Europe. Subsequent to this, some actual European paper folds were handed down, the most prominent being the pajarita (see page 94) and multiform.

In around 1880 travelers from the East introduced the flapping bird (see page 100) and the frog (see page 102). The German educator Friedrich Froebel (1782–1852) founded his kindergarten system in 1835, a part of which included European paper-folding, mainly based on geometric decorative folds. Froebel was building on the European tradition of paper-folding that was then prevalent.

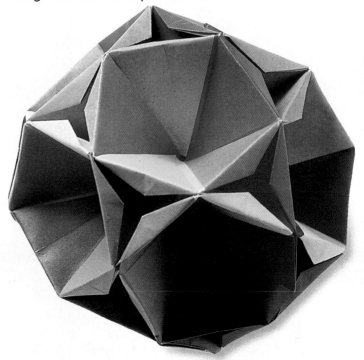

Paper-folding became a popular children's pastime in Victorian England, and John Tenniel's famous illustrations for *Through the Looking Glass*, by Lewis Carroll, feature two simple paper hats, one worn by the carpenter and the other, folded like a traditional boat, worn by the man dressed in white paper in the railroad carriage. A depiction of a similarly folded hat can also be found in the detailed painting *A Little Nimrod*, by James Joseph Jacques Tissot (a French painter), of around 1882.

A major popularization of origami was generated during the 1950s by Gershon Legman and Lilian Oppenheimer in the United States, and Robert Harbin in the U.K. Between Harbin, Samuel Randlett (U.S.A.), and Akira Yoshizawa of Japan, an international categorization of the symbols used in step diagrams to explain folding methods was developed. That system is still in use today. Harbin was a successful stage magician and traveled extensively, including to Japan, where he was exposed to the Eastern folding tradition.

Since then technical advances in the West have enormously increased the possibilities of models. Neil

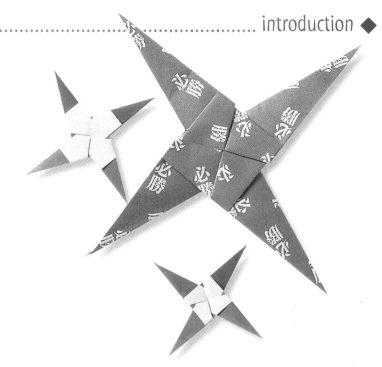

Elias (U.S.A.) gave us box pleating, while Robert Lang (U.S.A.) and John Montroll (U.S.A.) have greatly extended the range of bases and the complexity of models. Though the style may not please everyone, the detailed models now produced are undoubtedly technically far superior to earlier works.

What can be demonstrated is that origami still holds a special attraction. It is not only children who marvel at the transformation of an ordinary flat sheet of paper into something unexpected.

how to use this book

This book is intended as an introduction for beginners to the art of origami, although it will almost certainly be of interest to curious experts as well! The first chapter looks at the basic folds and bases that you will use for most of the models in this book, together with the principal symbols. The projects are roughly divided into groups, with each project being graded according to difficulty, and with projects increasing in difficulty through each chapter.

Work through this book gradually. There is no prize for finishing in double-quick time, so stay relaxed and don't set yourself ambitious targets.

How to "Read" Each Step

Use the "Understand-Do-Compare" method. Look at the first step. Work out what is meant to happen. Make the move. Compare the result with the second step. If they agree, repeat the process with the second step and compare the result with the third step and so forth. If they do not agree, unfold and try again. Consult the symbols to check your understanding. Use all of the information, noting the symbols used, the color, and so on.

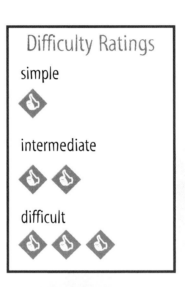

Difficulty Ratings

simple

intermediate

difficult

Although inexpensive, one-color paper is best when you begin origami; patterned and textured papers provide a decorative finishing touch to your models when you are more experienced. These can be obtained generally via specialist stockists. Check with your local or national society if you are uncertain.

The Symbols Used in Origami are Recognized the World Over

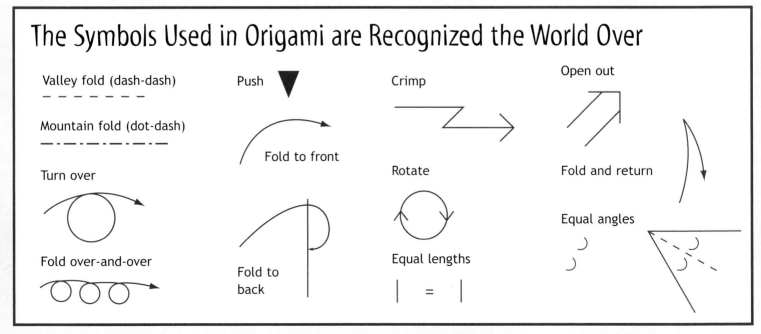

Valley fold (dash-dash)

Mountain fold (dot-dash)

Turn over

Fold over-and-over

Push

Fold to front

Fold to back

Crimp

Rotate

Equal lengths

Open out

Fold and return

Equal angles

Accuracy

The more accurately you fold, the better the shape of the final model, but please don't get hung up on absolute accuracy. The best approach is to fold freely, then, when the steps are familiar, to try to improve the accuracy. The second attempt is invariably better than the first, and the third is most likely better still. The whole point is to enjoy the experience.

Paper

Any paper can be used for origami (the cheaper the better when practicing a new model!) Some models depend on a contrast between the two sides of the paper. It is best to use commercial paper for such models. Some models work best with foil-backed paper for stiffness. Choosing a suitable paper is part of the experience of origami. I recommend a plain paper to begin with, as location points can merge into the background on patterned paper.

Models

The models chosen utilize a wide variety of techniques. This is intended to give the reader a thorough grounding in the available techniques. If you persevere, then you should be ready to tackle any published model.

Final words –

enjoy yourself,

and happy folding

◆1 folds and bases

The following pages introduce the main folds and bases that you will need to use for the projects in this book. It is important that you take time to practice and learn these techniques, as this will make the models much easier to master. Once you have understood the principles behind these different procedures, you will be able to experiment with folds and details of your own, which will only add to your enjoyment of origami.

Folding a Horizontal Crease

First align the corners without creasing the paper. Trap the paper at the corners with one hand. Place a finger on the top edge and run it down the center of the paper. Flatten the bottom edge from the center outward. Take care that the top corners remain aligned.

Valley Fold

This simple fold is the basis for all origami models. For this fold you bring the bottom edge of the paper up to meet the top edge, then flatten the crease at the bottom.

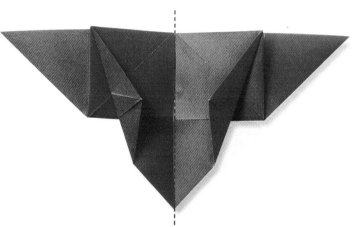

Folding a Diagonal Crease

Align the opposite corners without creasing the paper. Trap the top corners with one hand. Place a finger in the center and run it down the center of the paper. Flatten the bottom edge. Take care that the top corners remain aligned.

Mountain Fold

This is the opposite of the valley fold. Instead of folding the paper up and over, you need to fold one side of the paper underneath the other to make the two edges meet. This can be quite tricky, but there is nothing to stop you from turning the paper over and folding a valley, then turning the paper back again and reversing the fold.

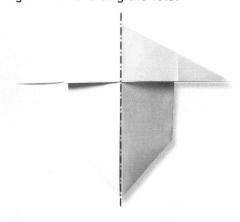

Rabbit-ear Fold

This fold creates a small, moveable flap. The name comes from the fact that it is a common fold to use when creating ears on a model. Here we start from a square sheet of paper with a diagonal fold.

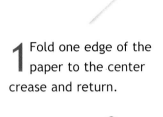

1 Fold one edge of the paper to the center crease and return.

2 Now fold the opposite edge to the center crease and again return.

3 Fold the two top edges together, using the previous two folds to find the center.

4 Now put in all of the creases firmly. Finally, fold the flap to one side.

5 This completes your rabbit-ear fold.

Squash

This fold may take some practice, as the squash is prone to scrunch up. Here we start with a rectangular sheet of paper, folded in half to make a square.

1 Valley-fold the top corner of the square and return.

2 Now take the edge of the paper to the crease and valley-fold. Return.

3 Separate the layers and apply pressure to the top of the flap. Flatten the flap, making sure that it remains even.

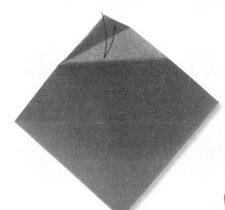

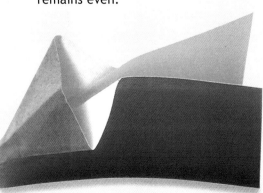

Squash Fold

A variation on the previous squash technique. This begins with the waterbomb base (see page 15).

1 Fold the left-hand edge to the center and return.

2 Bring this flap upright, separate the layers, and push down on the top edge.

3 Flatten the flap completely, taking care to keep it even.

Petal Fold

This fold uses the previous squash fold as a starting point.

1 Fold both corners of the squashed fold to the center and return.

2 Now fold these corners inside, using mountain folds, and lift the bottom point of the flap to meet the top.

3 Ensure that your creases are firm and even.

Inside Reverse Fold

Reverse folds are so called because you have to reverse, or change the direction of, some of your first creases. An inside reverse fold places the fold inside the main part of your paper. Here we start with a square sheet of paper, with a diagonal fold.

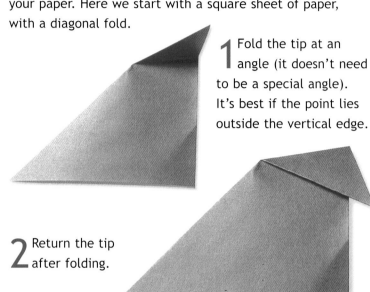

1 Fold the tip at an angle (it doesn't need to be a special angle). It's best if the point lies outside the vertical edge.

2 Return the tip after folding.

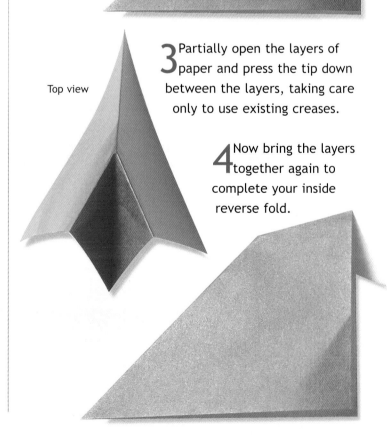

Top view

3 Partially open the layers of paper and press the tip down between the layers, taking care only to use existing creases.

4 Now bring the layers together again to complete your inside reverse fold.

Outside Reverse Fold

The principle is the same as for the inside reverse fold, except that the fold is outside the main part of the paper. We again start with a square sheet, folded diagonally.

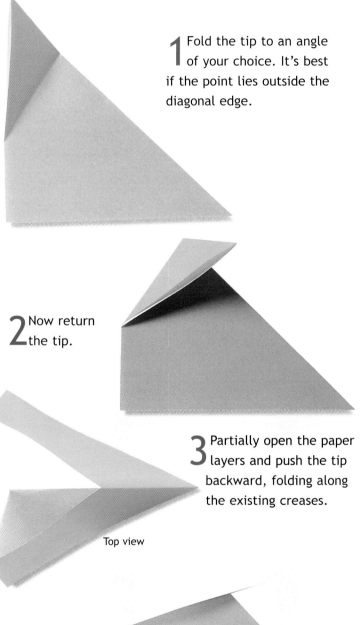

1 Fold the tip to an angle of your choice. It's best if the point lies outside the diagonal edge.

2 Now return the tip.

Top view

3 Partially open the paper layers and push the tip backward, folding along the existing creases.

4 Bring the layers together again. This is the completed outside reverse fold.

Outside Crimp

Crimping brings an extra fold to the principles of reversing. Here we start with a kite base (see page 14), mountain-folded in half.

1 Valley-fold the tip to any angle.

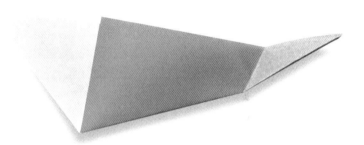

2 Now valley-fold the tip in the opposite direction and unfold.

3 Refold using the existing creases, reversing the crease direction in the far side. This fold is used to form heads and feet.

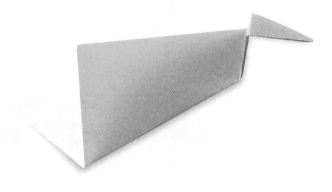

Inside Crimp

This crimp gain begins with a kite base (see below), mountain-folded in half.

1 Valley-fold the tip to the desired angle.

2 Valley-fold the tip in the opposite direction.

3 Unfold and then refold, using existing creases. The direction needs to be reversed on the front.

Preliminary base

Here all four corners of a square meet. The starting point is a square sheet with a diagonal crease.

1 Mountain-fold the top corner to the bottom corner and return. Now valley-fold the top left edge to the bottom right edge. Finally, valley-fold the top right edge to the bottom left edge.

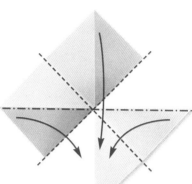

2 Bring all four corners of the sheet together and flatten along the creases.

Kite Base

So called because its shape resembles a kite, this is the easiest of all bases. Start with a square sheet of paper with a diagonal crease.

Fold both sides of the sheet to meet the center line. Once both edges are evenly lined up, make the creases firmly.

Blintz Base

Also called "blintzing." This procedure gets its name from a Jewish pastry! The starting point is a square with two diagonal creases.

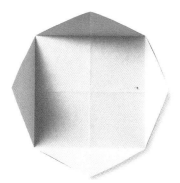 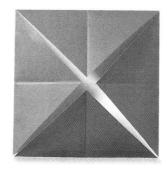

1 Valley-fold each corner of the square to the center point – marked where the two diagonal creases meet.

2 Fold your creases firmly and evenly.

Waterbomb Base

As its name suggests, this forms the basis for the waterbomb model shown on page 34. Here we start with a square valley folded from left to right.

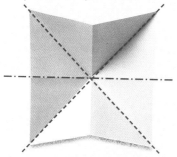 

1 Mountain-fold the top edge to the bottom. Diagonally valley-fold the top left-hand corner to the bottom right-hand corner. Finally, diagonally valley-fold the top right-hand corner to the bottom left-hand corner.

2 Gently push the creases toward the center to create a star shape. Then flatten the paper to give two tips on each side.

Windmill Base

So called because of the shape that it creates, this is a very versatile base. Its begins with a square sheet creased in half both ways.

1 Valley-fold the top edge to the center line. Now valley-fold the bottom edge to the center line.

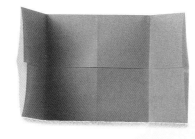

2 Fold both ends to the center crease.

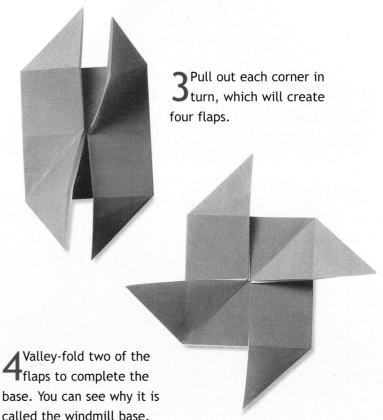

3 Pull out each corner in turn, which will create four flaps.

4 Valley-fold two of the flaps to complete the base. You can see why it is called the windmill base.

Fish Base

This is another versatile base. Here we begin with a square sheet, creased diagonally in half both ways.

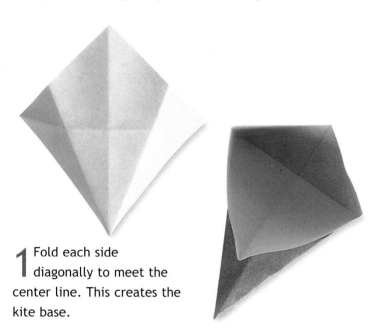

1 Fold each side diagonally to meet the center line. This creates the kite base.

2 Fold the top tip behind to meet the bottom tip. Make the mountain and valley folds as shown.

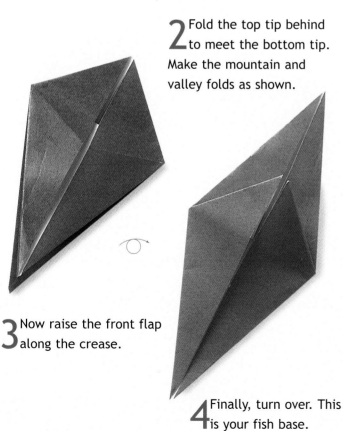

3 Now raise the front flap along the crease.

4 Finally, turn over. This is your fish base.

Bird Base

This base can be quite complicated, and forms the basis of many projects. The starting point is the preliminary base, closed end at top.

1 Valley-fold the left and right corners to the center and return. Mountain-fold the top tip to the back and return.

2 Lift the bottom flap of the top layer only and bring it to the top.

3 This is what the model should look like at this stage.

4 Turn the model over. Fold the middle flap up.

5 Lift the bottom flap of the top layer only and take it to the top.

6 Now fold down the top tips of both the top and bottom layers.

7 The completed bird base.

Stretched Bird Base

This is a variation on the previous bird base.

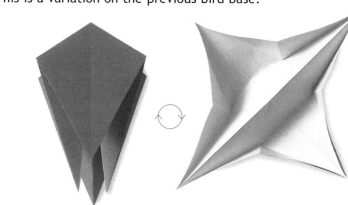

1 It begins with the conventional completed bird base.

2 Rotate the base. Pull the inner flaps until the bottom point pops inside.

3 Then flatten the paper to complete.

Blintz Bird Base

Here we begin with a square sheet folded in half in both directions. Note that, unlike the previous bases, the colored side of the paper is face up.

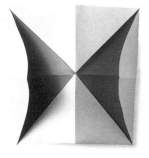

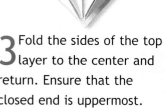

1 Fold the four corners to the center.

2 Form the preliminary base, with the loose flaps outermost.

3 Fold the sides of the top layer to the center and return. Ensure that the closed end is uppermost.

4 Petal-fold, front and back. The upper layer is lifted and the sides follow.

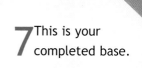

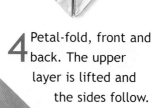

5 Now pull out the hidden corners.

6 Fold the flaps down at both the front and back.

7 This is your completed base.

Frog Base

This is quite a complex base that will need plenty of practice to ensure accuracy.

1 Form the preliminary base (see page 14).

2 Squash the right-hand tip of the top layer (see page 11 for full squash instructions).

3 Swing the flap you've created to the other side using existing creases.

4 Now squash the left-hand tip of the top layer in the same way.

5 Make sure that all of your creases are firm and even.

6 Turn the model over. Now squash the right-hand tip as before.

7 Swing this flap to the other side.

8 Squash the left-hand tip as before.

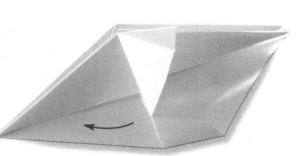

9 Now valley-fold the edges to the center and return. Ensure that the creases go exactly to point. Now raise the top layer on a line joining the folded edges and petal-fold (see page 12).

10 This model shows the petal-fold partway.

11 Finally, repeat the petal fold on three more flaps to complete the frog base.

Sink Fold

This can be quite difficult to follow, as it combines several valley and mountain folds. It is important to make sure that your folds are all in the correct place. This begins with a square sheet, folded in half horizontally.

1 First form the waterbomb base (see page 15), with the color on the outside.

2 Fold the tip to the center of the bottom edge, crease firmly, and return. Turn over and repeat. This will mark your creases.

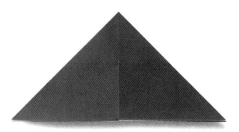

3 Open out your sheet and examine the creases.

4 Work round the sheet, putting in mountain folds in the outer corners and mountain folds in the central square.

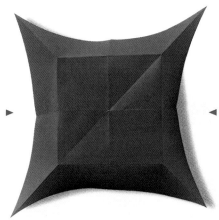

5 Push down in the center, while at the same time pushing the sides at the middle.

6 Continue to push down and bring the corners together. Take time to line up the folds precisely.

Bottom view

7 This is the completed sink. You can see that the top triangle in step 2 lies inside the layers, i.e., it is "sunk."

Double Sink Fold

A variation on the previous fold, which, as its name suggests, doubles the number of folds used. This again begins with a square sheet, folded in half horizontally.

1 Form the waterbomb base (page 15); the color should be on the outside.

2 Fold the tip to the center of the bottom edge, crease firmly, and return. Turn over and repeat step 2.

3 Fold the tip to the crease, crease firmly, and return. Turn over and repeat this step.

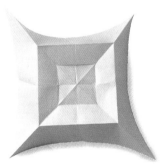

4 Open out the sheet and work round, putting mountain folds in the outer corners and the outer central square.

5 Push down in the center, while pushing the sides from the center, and bring the corners together.

6 Partially open out to the previous step. This is the single sink.

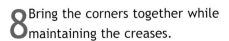

7 Push the center up to form the creases illustrated.

8 Bring the corners together while maintaining the creases.

9 This is the completed fold. The top triangles in step 3 are "sunk."

❷ basic models

The first projects are some of the simplest to create and will allow you to gain confidence in your folding before moving on to some of the more complex models.

dart

This is one of the easiest models to make, and is one which many people make without even realizing they're creating an origami model! No special paper is required, as any sheet of paper measuring around 8 x 12in (21 x 30cm) is perfectly suitable.

1 Bring the long edges together, crease, and unfold.

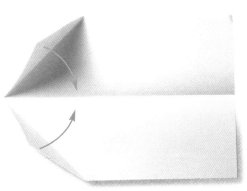

2 Bring the short edges to the center crease, using diagonal valley folds.

3 Bring the folded edges to the center crease, again using valley folds. Ensure that the already folded corners do not creep.

4 Fold the model in half, hiding the folds.

5 Fold down the wings at right angles. Ensure that you make the folds in the same place on each side.

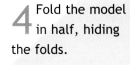

banger

A traditional model much loved by schoolchildren! Again, a sheet of paper measuring around 8 x 12in (21 x 30cm) is ideal; the paper needs to be thin, but strong.

1 Crease both the horizontal and vertical center lines and return.

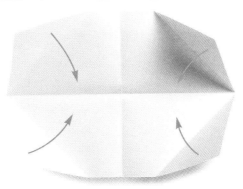

2 Fold the corners down to the longer center line.

3 Fold the model in half with a valley fold. The corners are inside.

4 Now fold the top corners to the center line.

5 Fold the model in half again, this time with a mountain fold.

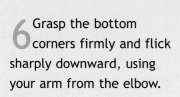

6 Grasp the bottom corners firmly and flick sharply downward, using your arm from the elbow.

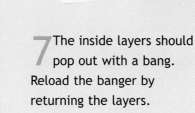

7 The inside layers should pop out with a bang. Reload the banger by returning the layers.

boat/snapper

Two models in one! Another design that can be easily folded using a sheet of paper measuring 8 x 12in (21 x 30cm). We start with a rectangle with a central vertical fold.

1 Fold the sheet horizontally.

2 Now fold the two top corners down to the center line.

3 Fold the bottom edge of the top layer up to the top as far as possible. Make sure that you keep this even. Repeat with the back layer.

4 Pull the layers apart and flatten the model.Fold the bottom point of the top layer up to meet the top point. Repeat with the back layer.

5 Pull these layers apart and flatten.

6 Fold the bottom point of the top layer to meet the top point. Repeat with the back layer.

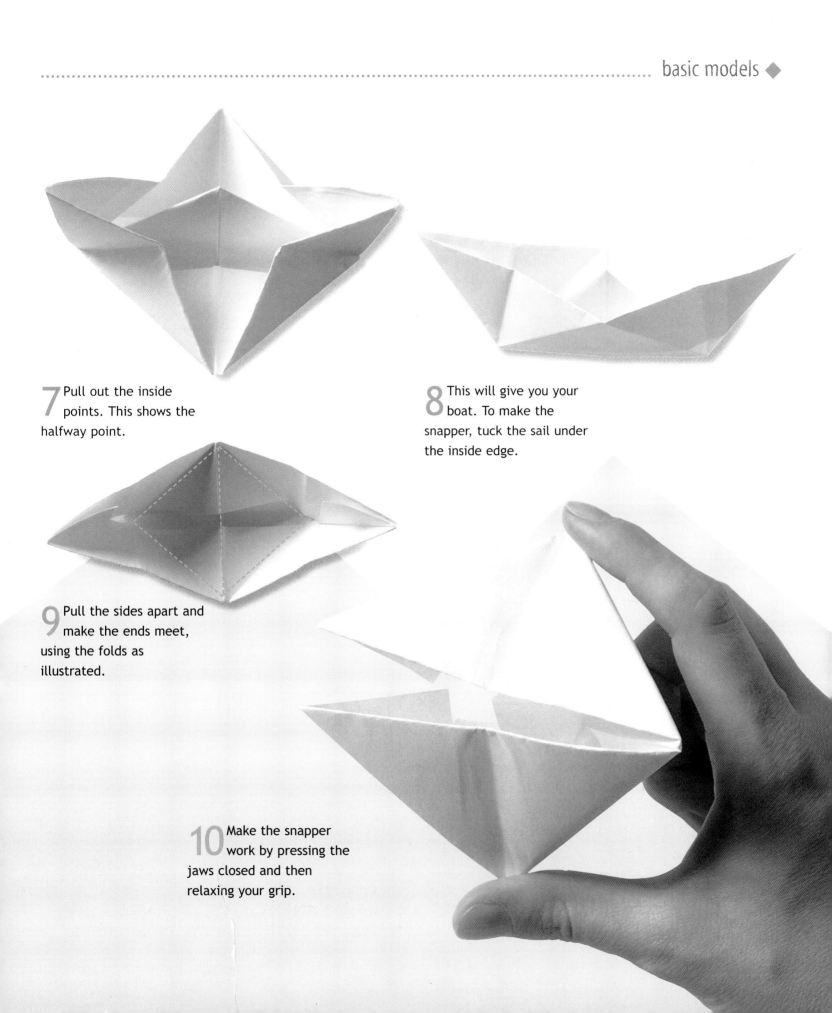

7 Pull out the inside points. This shows the halfway point.

8 This will give you your boat. To make the snapper, tuck the sail under the inside edge.

9 Pull the sides apart and make the ends meet, using the folds as illustrated.

10 Make the snapper work by pressing the jaws closed and then relaxing your grip.

House

This design can be made using any size origami paper. The house can be decorated by drawing in windows and doors if you wish. It begins with a square with a vertical crease. As with most models, the white side of the paper is face up.

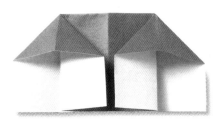

1 Fold the origami paper in half horizontally.

2 Fold the short edges to the centre.

3 Open the top layer and squash the top corners.

Organ

A fun model that begins with the completed house model. This can also be decorated by drawing in keys if you wish.

1 Fold up the central section of the house so that the edge meets the top edge.

2 Crease this folded section, lifting up white area, and return.

3 Fold the top edge of this section down to meet the crease you created in step 2.

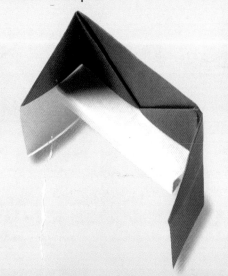

4 Now fold along the crease made in step 2.

5 Fold the sides at right angles. Now fold the 'keyboard' down at right angles too.

house envelope

An original design that follows on from the house model. It involves lots of quite small folds, so to begin with at least you may wish to practise this on larger origami paper. It begins with a square, creased vertically in half.

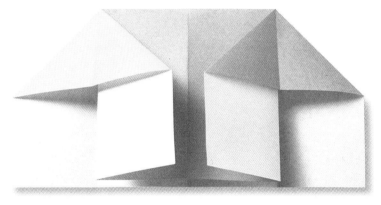

1 Fold the square horizontally in half.

2 Fold the sides to the centre and squash the top corners.

3 Fold the flaps you've created to the outside, trapping the coloured triangles between the layers.

4 Now fold the bottom edges up to the centre.

5 Fold the top edges down. Ensure that the corners are free.

6 Fold the flaps in towards the middle, using existing creases.

continued ▶

7 Fold the bottom flap up and tuck it in.

8 Now fold the sides into the center.

9 Fold the bottom corners into the center.

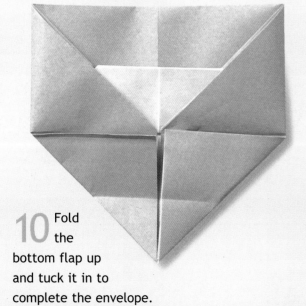

10 Fold the bottom flap up and tuck it in to complete the envelope.

◆3 containers

The projects in this chapter include a variety of different boxes, from the very simple to the more complicated, as well as some more unusual containers.

simple box

This box is called *masu* in Japanese, which means "measuring box." It may require some practice to make the sides even, but you will have a pretty display box.

1 Crease the square in half both vertically and horizontally and return.

2 Fold each corner to the center – you have created the blintz base.

3 Fold all sides to the center and return.

4 Now open the two opposite corners of the blintz base.

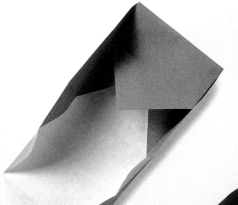

5 Lift the sides so that they are vertical.

6 Now lift one of the remaining ends. This brings the model into three dimensions. Fold the flap at the raised end into the center. It traps the colored triangles.

7 Raise the remaining end and fold the flap of this end into the center. You may have to firm up your creases to finish off.

multibox

Another traditional display box, which gets its name from the multiplicity of rectangles that it can be folded from.

1 Crease the vertical center line.

2 Fold the left- and right-hand edges to the center line.

3 Fold back a strip of each flap.

4 Now fold both strips back again.

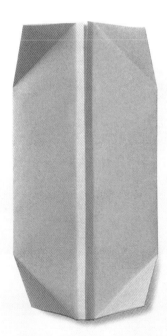

5 Fold each of the four corners to the crease that is formed by folding the strips.

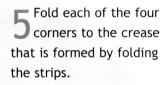

6 Now fold back the strip on each flap, trapping the corners.

7 Lift the layers on each side to open the box. You may need to firm up the creases to make a sharp box shape.

house box

This project uses the ever-versatile house model as its basis. It begins with a square sheet, creased horizontally in half. The colored side of the paper should be face up.

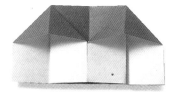

1 Mountain-fold the square in half, retaining the color on the outside.

2 Fold the sides to the center and squash the top corners.

3 Fold the flaps to the outside, trapping the triangles in the layers.

4 Fold the bottom edges to the center. Repeat on both sides.

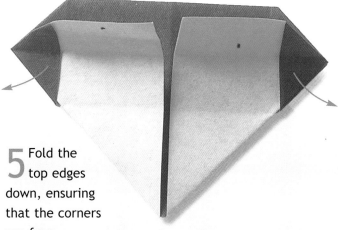

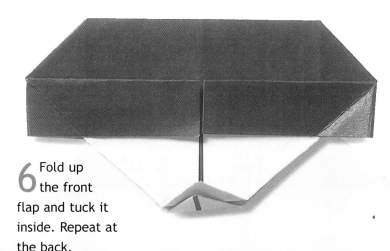

5 Fold the top edges down, ensuring that the corners are free.

6 Fold up the front flap and tuck it inside. Repeat at the back.

7 Press on the ridge at the top and pull into three dimensions. Now turn over.

drinking cup

This model can be made in any size, and, like the drinking cup after which it is named, will actually hold water, although probably not for very long!

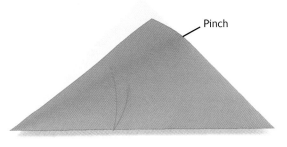

Pinch

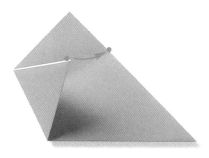

1 First fold the square diagonally, using a valley fold.

2 Take the top flap down to the bottom edge, but pinch only at the edge and do not crease.

3 Take the left-hand corner to the pinch on the right-hand edge so that the marked points meet.

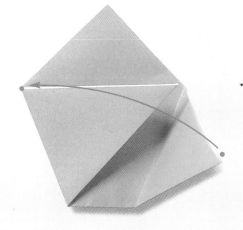

4 Now take the right-hand corner to the left-hand end so that the marked points meet.

5 Fold the upper corner of the top layer down to the front.

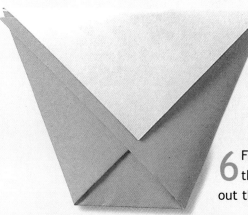

6 Fold the remaining upper flap to the rear. Use your finger to open out the cup.

difficulty :

origin :
traditional

waterbomb

The waterbomb is a classic traditional design and one that will be familiar to many people. It is probably better to practise making it using larger paper to give yourself room to make all of the folds neatly.

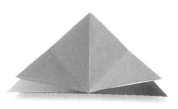

1 Fold both diagonals and return. Turn over.

2 Fold the horizontal and vertical centre lines and then return.

3 Turn the paper over and then collapse it along the creases.

4 Fold the tips of the top layer to the top. Repeat at the rear.

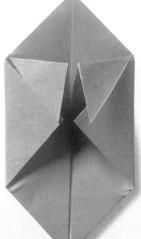

7 Now fold and tuck these flaps into the little pockets that you've created. Gently press on the edge to open the pockets. Repeat at the rear.

5 Fold the left- and right-hand corners to the centre. Repeat at the rear.

6 Fold the top tips down. Now repeat at the rear.

8 Separate the layers and blow into the hole at the bottom. You may find it helpful to fold and return the top and bottom points at the centre to ease the final shaping.

complex box .... containers ◆

We have already seen a simple box construction. However, once you have mastered the simple box, you may enjoy the number of complex folds in this variation. It begins with the paper's coloured side face up.

  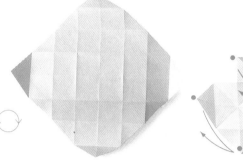 

1 Crease the diagonals and blintz in and return all four corners.

2 Crease and return the corners to meet the blintz creases.

3 Turn the paper over. Fold and return the left- and right-hand corners to meet your original blintz creases. Fold in the top and bottom corners to meet the blintzed creases. Then fold the top and bottom edges along the blintz creases so that the edge lies along the crease that forms the central square.

4 Crease the top left-hand edge along the imaginary line formed between the bottom left-hand corner of the top coloured band and the bottom of the left-hand crease you created in step 3. Repeat on the other three edges.

 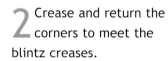

5 Turn the paper over. Fold the sides at right angles and waterbomb the ends (see page 15 for instructions).

6 Squash the folds at either side. Turn over.

7 Tuck the tips into the pocket nearest to the centre of the box.

sanbow

To the Japanese, the sanbow is an offering tray. It is a complex model to make, but the result is a delicate and decorative box.

1 First crease and return both diagonal center lines. Then create a blintz base, colored side out (see page 15), turn over, and mountain-fold in half.

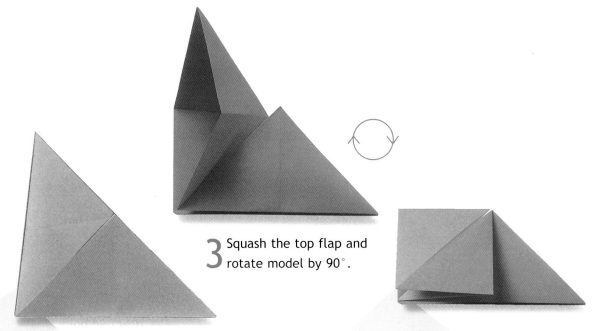

2 Now valley-fold the flap up to a right angle.

3 Squash the top flap and rotate model by 90°.

4 This will give you a right-hand flap.

5 Turn the model over and again fold the flap up to a right angle.

6 Now squash the top flap.

7 Lift the front corner up, opening out the side flaps as you do so.

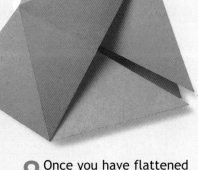

8 Once you have flattened out the flaps, turn the model over.

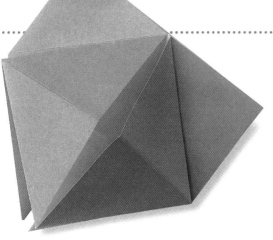

9 Lift the front flap and open out the side flaps as in step 7.

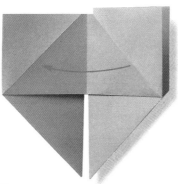

10 Fold the top right layer over to the left. Now turn over and do the same at the rear. This is a book fold.

11 Now fold both sides in to the center line, front and rear.

12 Rotate the model so that the point is at the top. Fold down the top front flap so that the point meets the bottom edge. Repeat at the rear.

13 Pull the front and rear flaps out to open out the sanbow.

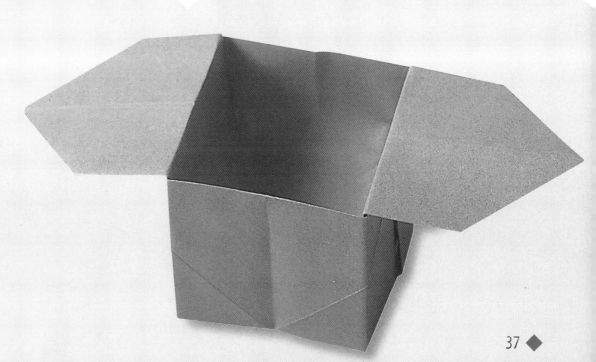

lazy susan

A lazy Susan is a food-serving container. It was so called because the dish provided a way of storing several items ready for visitors, thus saving time. This is an unusual model in that it has curved sides.

1 With the colored side of the paper face up, crease the center lines horizontally and vertically.

2 Now crease both diagonal center lines.

3 Now fold in all four corners to the center to create a blintz.

4 Fold the four corners to the outside edges.

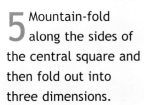

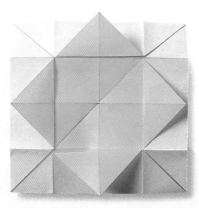

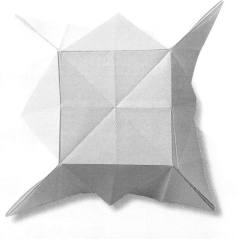

5 Mountain-fold along the sides of the central square and then fold out into three dimensions.

6 Push the center downward, and at the same time push the sides inward.

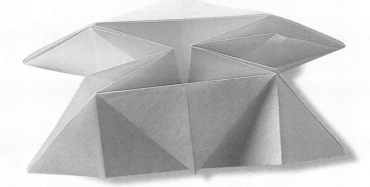

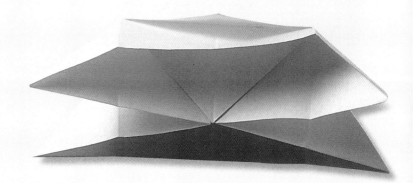

7 This is the shape that you should finish up with.

8 Inside reverse-fold both of the front tips.

9 Now inside reverse-fold both of the back tips.

10 This is how your model should look at this stage.

11 Push in the bottom with a curved fold and separate the layers. Repeat on all four sides. Neaten the inner pockets to form a star shape.

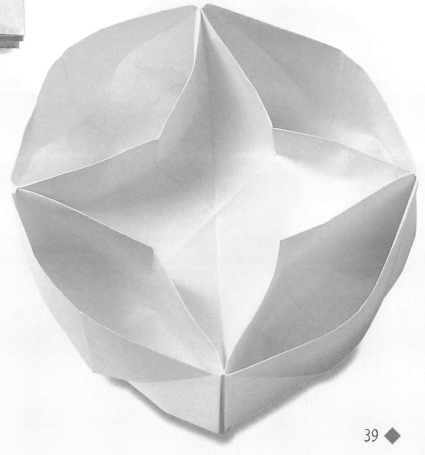

4 novelty models

These models are particularly fun to make, and with a little experimentation with folds and use of color you can create your own variations.

japanese helmet .... novelty models ◆

A simple, yet effective, design that creates the traditional Japanese warrior's helmet. It can be combined with the head model shown on page 46 or the page-marker base on pages 52-53 for a different effect.

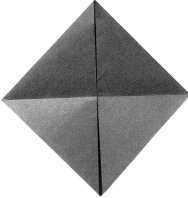

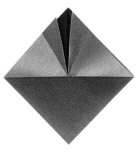

1 Fold the paper in half along the diagonal.

2 Fold down both top corners to meet the bottom corner.

3 Now fold these new bottom corners up to meet the top corner.

4 Next fold the front tips outward.

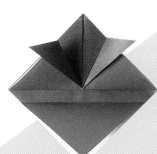

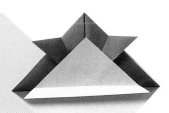

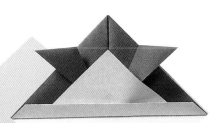

5 Fold up the bottom corner of the top layer, as illustrated above.

6 Next fold up the edge of this new flap.

7 Fold up the remaining flap and tuck it inside.

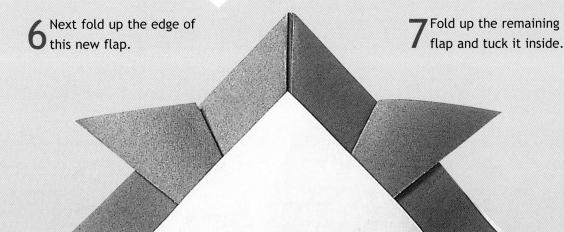

yakko-san

Another traditional design from Japan, this can be decorated with a face if you wish. It may be a good idea to use larger-sized paper for this model.

1 Crease both the horizontal and the vertical center lines.

2 Fold all four corners into the center.

3 This creates the first blintz base.

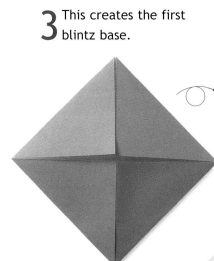

4 Turn the paper over. Fold all four corners into the center again.

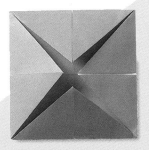

5 This creates the second blintz base.

6 Turn over. Fold the four corners into the center once more.

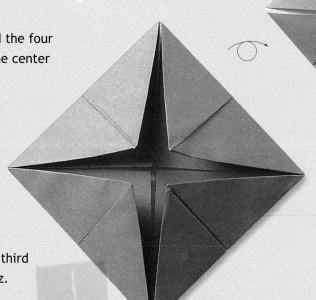

7 This creates a third and final blintz.

8 Turn over. Now fold the inner corner out and return.

9 Fold the inner corner out, and this time pull out the colored triangles.

10 Repeat steps 8 and 9 on two more corners to complete the model.

japanese lady

This is a pretty model that can be adapted to create any number of figures. The model is made in two stages: the kimono and the head. Using special patterned paper can provide a particularly appealing effect.

kimono

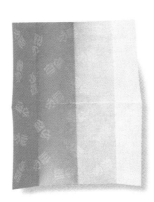

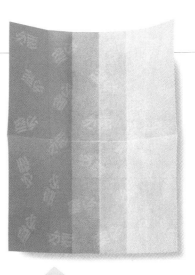

1 Crease both the horizontal and the vertical center lines.

2 Fold both the left-hand and the right-hand edges into the center and return.

3 Make a valley fold halfway between the center crease and the left-hand crease and return. Repeat on the right-hand side.

4 Pleat to the center along these creases. The outer creases should be valley folds, while the inner creases are mountain folds.

5 Fold the model in half from front to back using a mountain fold.

6 Fold the front layer on both sides to the center and then squash the top corners.

7 Mountain-fold the back flap upward along the line of the bottom of the white tirangles.

8 Your model should now look like this. Turn it over.

9 Swivel the flaps down. There should be a valley crease in the white underlayer.

10 This is your completed kimono.

head

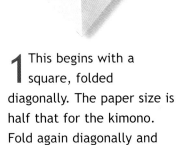

1 This begins with a square, folded diagonally. The paper size is half that for the kimono. Fold again diagonally and then return.

2 Fold the top corner down by approximately one-quarter of the length of the paper.

3 Fold in the top edges. The top corners lie on the side of the colored triangle.

4 This is the result. Now turn the model over.

5 Fold both sides to the center line.

6 Now turn your model over once more.

7 This is the completed head. Combine it with the kimono for the finished model.

pencil

.... novelty models ◆

You can make a whole set of colored pencils to display using this fun and simple design. This model uses a rectangle four times longer than its width (4 x 1). For a longer pencil, use 6 x 1 or 8 x 1 paper.

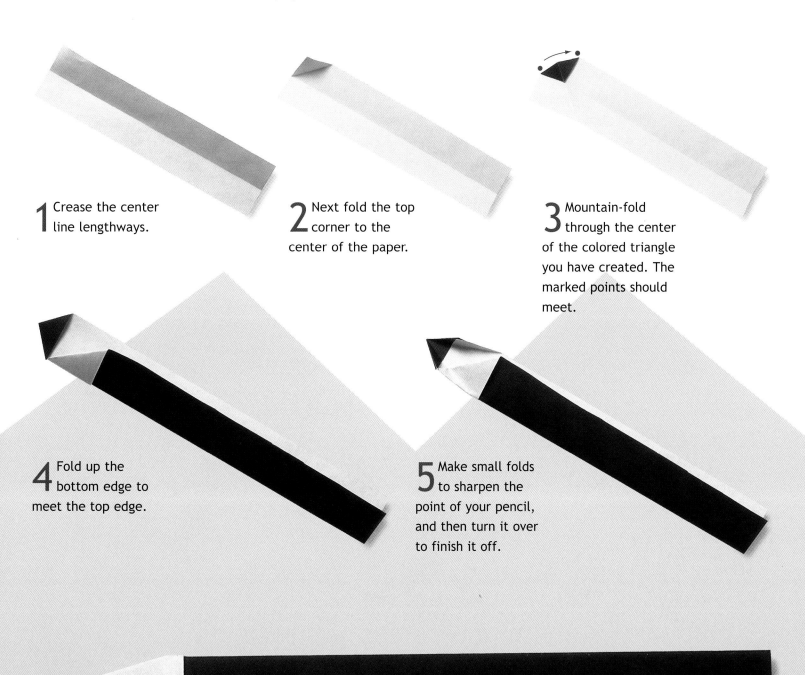

1 Crease the center line lengthways.

2 Next fold the top corner to the center of the paper.

3 Mountain-fold through the center of the colored triangle you have created. The marked points should meet.

4 Fold up the bottom edge to meet the top edge.

5 Make small folds to sharpen the point of your pencil, and then turn it over to finish it off.

soccer gear

This is a fun design based on a traditional model. You can use any colored paper you like to create shirts and shorts in any soccer team's colors. It consists of two models: a shirt and shorts. The shirt requires a rectangle of paper twice as long as it is wide. The shorts require a square, which may need to be trimmed to fit.

shirt

1 Crease the rectangle into quarters vertically. Valley-fold the two bottom corners and then fold a small strip at the top to the rear.

2 Crease and return the bottom corners and then fold the sides into the center.

3 Fold the top to the rear. Fold the bottom to the rear and return.

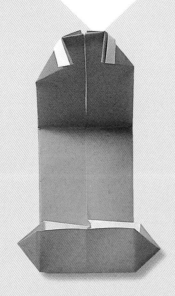

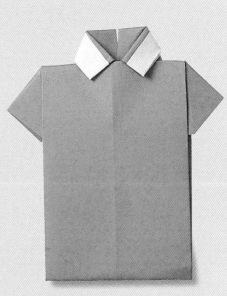

4 Pull out the bottom flaps. Fold the top corners to the middle.

5 Fold up the bottom to the top, tucking the edge under the collar tips.

6 This is your completed shirt.

shorts

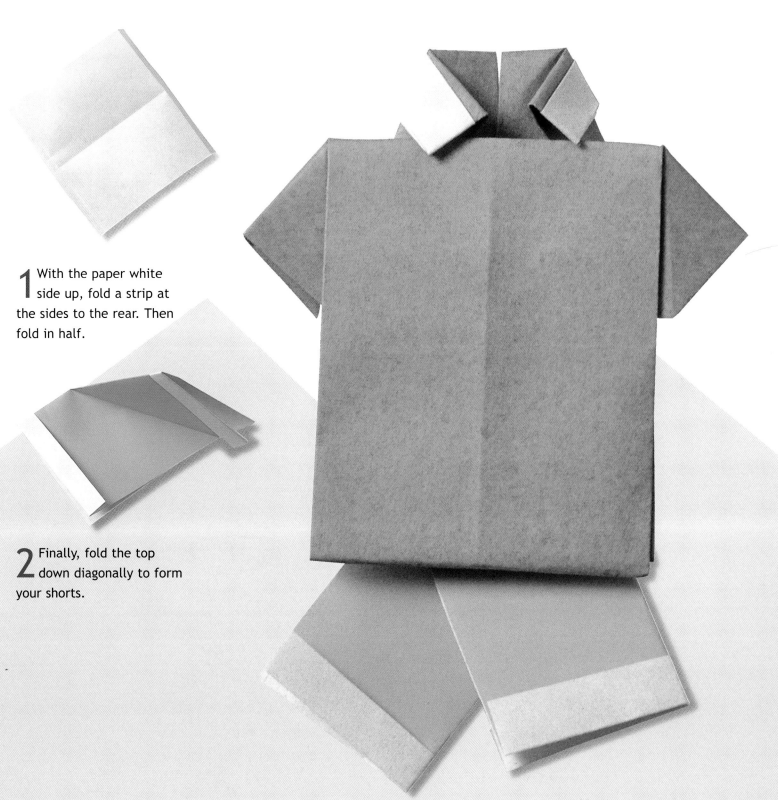

1 With the paper white side up, fold a strip at the sides to the rear. Then fold in half.

2 Finally, fold the top down diagonally to form your shorts.

paintbrush

This is a relatively simple model, but care must be taken to make the folds accurate.

The model requires a strip of 4 x 1 paper. It begins with the colored side face up.

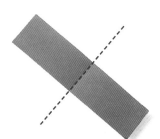

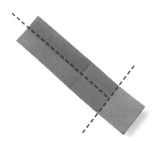

1 First crease a vertical center line.

2 To the left of this center line, fold and return a horizontal center line. To the right of the original center line, fold and return another vertical center line.

3 Between the two vertical center lines, fold and return another vertical center line.

4 Pleat the right-hand edge to the center crease created in step 3.

5 Mountain-fold this edge to the rear on the center line.

6 Mountain-fold the top and bottom edges inside. Squash the corners.

7 Fold the long flap at the left out to the right.

8 Fold the right-hand edge to meet the imaginary line formed between the inside corners of the main shape.

9 Fold the long sides to the center and squash the left-hand corners.

10 Round the handle of the brush by blunting the corners. Fold in the top and bottom edges of the brush head.

difficulty :

origin :
david petty

page markers

Once you have mastered the art of making the page-marker base, you can create a variety of different figures – just use your imagination. Here we show two examples. The page-marker base requires a strip of 4 x 1 paper.

page-marker base

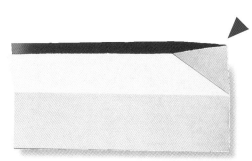

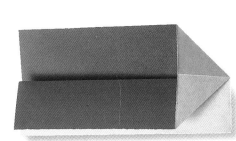

1 With the colored side face up, fold the strip in half lengthways.

2 Fold the top layer vertically and squash the top right-hand corner.

3 This is the result that you should end up with.

4 Turn the model over. Once again, fold the top layer vertically and squash the top right-hand corner.

5 Fold the edges to the center and return. Repeat at the rear. Return the edges to the center and inside reverse-fold the four corners.

6 Fold the bottom strip to the top. Turn over and repeat at the rear. This is called a book fold.

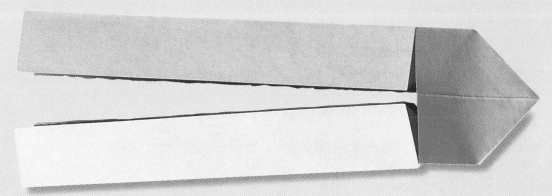

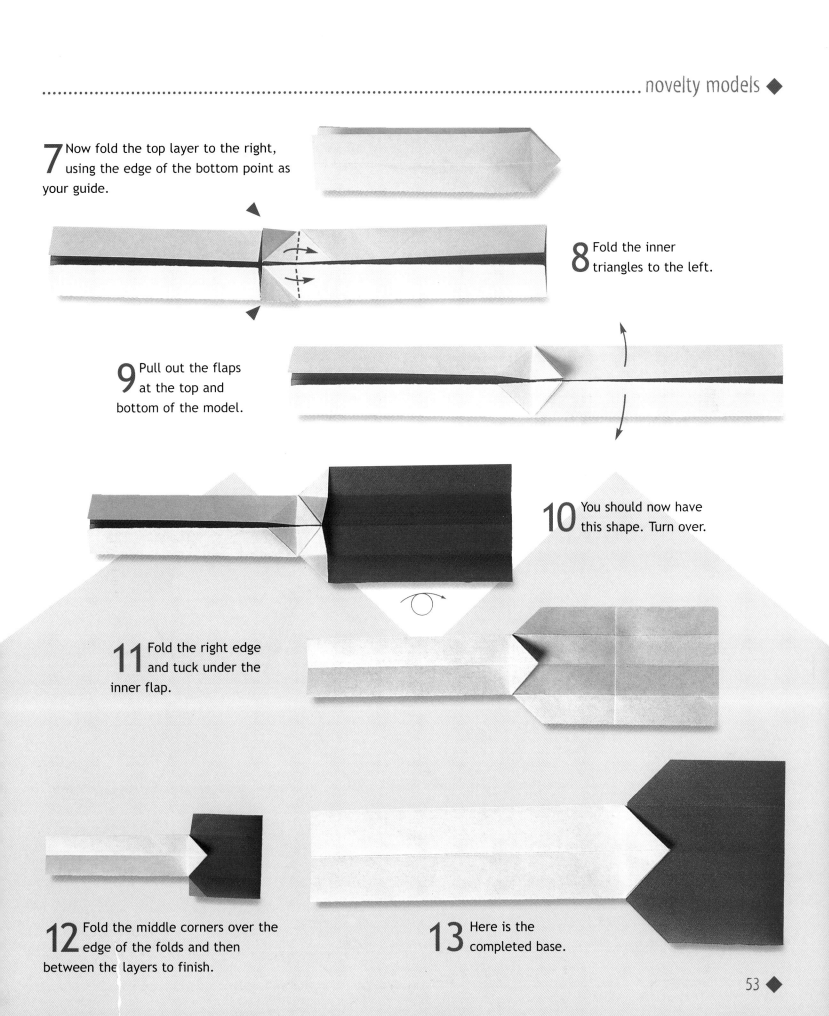

7 Now fold the top layer to the right, using the edge of the bottom point as your guide.

8 Fold the inner triangles to the left.

9 Pull out the flaps at the top and bottom of the model.

10 You should now have this shape. Turn over.

11 Fold the right edge and tuck under the inner flap.

12 Fold the middle corners over the edge of the folds and then between the layers to finish.

13 Here is the completed base.

santa page marker

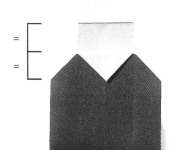

2 Fold out the flap and squash the corners at the top.

4 This is the result you should end up with.

1 Begin with the page-marker base. Fold the top of the base to the rear, folding slightly above the colored points.

3 Fold up a short strip at the bottom.

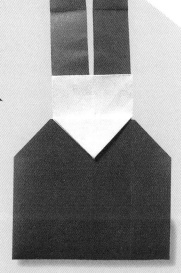

5 Turn the model over and then fold the sides to the center.

6 Fold up the front flap, folding at the line where the color and the top white strip meet.

7 This should be the result. Turn the model over once more.

8 Fold down the top flap so that it overlaps the white edge in the middle.

9 Tuck the top edge of the white center shape inside the white edge you have just folded down. (You may find it easier to fold in the top corners of the strip to be tucked in).

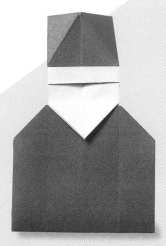

10 Fold the top corners behind the model to complete Santa's hat.

nurse page marker

1 Start with a page-marker base, with the color reversed.

2 Fold under the bottom tip of the colored band. Turn the model over.

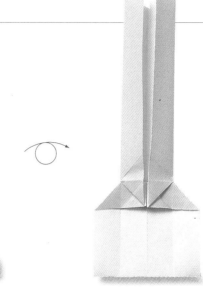

3 Fold out the flaps at the top and squash the corners at the bottom.

4 Fold the top flap down and the sides in.

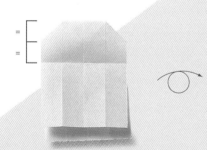

5 Fold the colored flap up and then turn the model over again.

6 Fold the top down and the sides in.

7 Fold the side flaps down and then tuck them inside to finish the model.

beating heart .... novelty models ◆

This is a fun, moving model that makes a heartbeat sound when pressed. You will need a 4 x 1 rectangle and should begin with the colored side face up.

1 Fold the strip of paper vertically in half.

2 Fold down the top folded corner to meet the bottom edge.

3 Squash this fold. (For instructions on squash-folding, see page 12.)

4 Petal-fold the squash you have just made. (See page 12 for full petal-fold instructions.)

5 Fold in the left-hand corners of the top layer. Repeat at the rear.

6 Now separate the layers of paper.

7 This shows the rear of the model.

8 Grasp the tab at the rear between your finger and thumb. Push into the center of the petal fold with your thumbnail. The heart will beat. Relax your thumb to reset it.

christmas lantern

This pretty, three-dimensional model makes an excellent tree decoration. It is another complex model, so will require both practice and patience. This begins with the preliminary base, closed end down.

1 Crease and return the top corner to meet the bottom corner, but do not fold. Make a pinch only. Fold and return the bottom corner to the pinch. Sink the bottom corner (for sink instructions, see page 19).

2 Fold both the left- and right-hand corners to the center line and return. Repeat at the rear.

3 Sink each of these four corners.

4 Fold the left point to the top point, crease, and return. Fold the left point to the bottom point, crease, and return. Repeat at the rear. Do the same on the hidden side flaps.

5 Fold down the top corner to the front, creasing along an imaginary line between the left- and right-hand corners. Repeat at rear. Do the same on the hidden side flaps.

6 Collapse the left- and right-hand flaps inward, using the existing creases. Repeat at the rear and also on the hidden side flaps.

7 Swing the left-hand flap you've created to the other side. Repeat at rear.

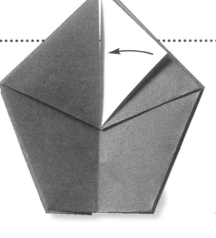

8 Fold the flap back along the center line.

9 Tuck the flap inside the pocket created in the colored section. Repeat at the rear.

10 Swing the remaining flap to the left. Now repeat at the rear.

11 Tuck this flap inside the right-hand colored pocket. Repeat at the rear. Perform steps 7–11 on the hidden side flaps.

12 Tuck under the middle flap, using a mountain fold. Repeat at the rear.

13 Pull up the four flaps at the top. Insert a finger into the base to maneuver the model into three dimensions and complete it.

3d heart

This is an attractive model that can be made into a pretty, handmade, pop-up card containing a special note. The card itself can be made from any type of colored card of your choice.

1 Crease both horizontal and vertical center lines and return.

2 Valley-fold the left- and right-hand corners to the center and return. Mountain-fold the bottom corner to the rear and then return again.

3 Crease the sheet into quarters. Do this by folding each of the edges to the center line. Return after folding.

4 Crease the top corner to meet the bottom crease and return. Crease the bottom corner upward to meet the bottom crease and return.

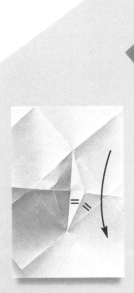

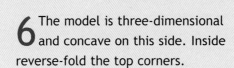

5 Crease two valleys and one mountain in the central top diamond, as illustrated, then fold.

6 The model is three-dimensional and concave on this side. Inside reverse-fold the top corners.

7 Inside reverse-fold the top corners. The fold should begin from the center of the square edge.

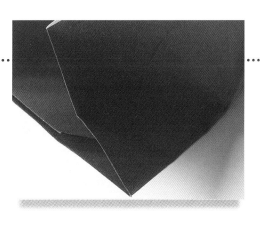

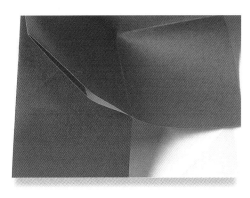

9 The tucking fold at the top can be tricky. Valley-fold the left-hand edge along the inner edge.

8 Make folds as shown to tuck the outer edges into the model.

10 Now fold in this corner along the inner edge and return.

11 Using the crease lines you have created, tuck the corner into the top pocket.

12 Tuck the top layer of the bottom corner into the pocket behind.

13 You can now slide a personalized note into this inner pocket if you wish. Turn the model over for the 3D heart.

14 You can also use the heart as the basis for a romantic card.

rocking santa

A festive model that makes an ideal Christmas decoration, particularly if you make several. This model begins with a square sheet folded diagonally through the center and with the colored side face up.

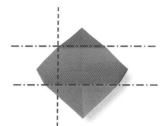

1 Crease a diagonal line, pinch it at the center, and return. Fold the right-hand corner to the center and then return.

2 Fold the left-hand corner to the crease. Mountain-fold the top and bottom corners to the rear.

3 Mountain-fold the model horizontally in half.

4 Squash the top right-hand corner.

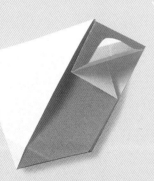

5 Fold the bottom corner of the top layer inside. Repeat at the rear. Fold the flap of the squashed fold back on itself several times. This forms Santa's hatband.

6 Fold the corners inside and repeat on the back layer. Rotate the model so that the white corner is at the rear. Santa will rock if he is nudged gently.

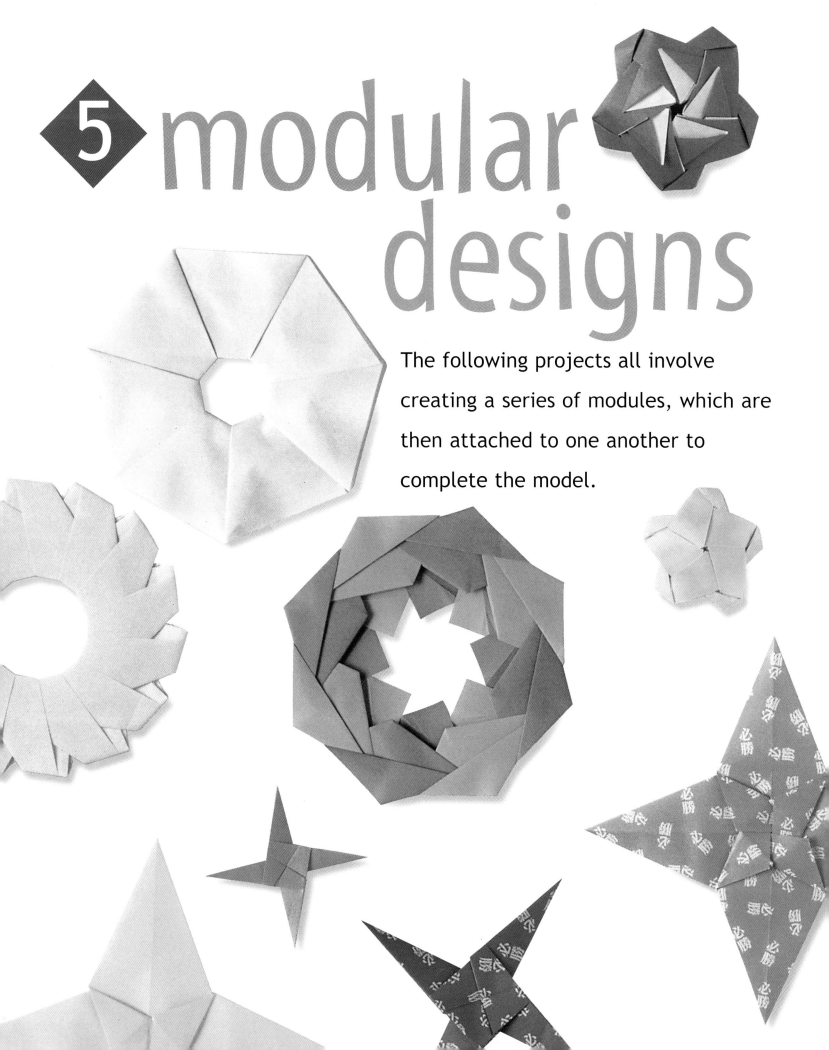

5 modular designs

The following projects all involve creating a series of modules, which are then attached to one another to complete the model.

difficulty :

origin :
david petty

napkin ring

A simple way to make unusual table decorations. You need to make five modules.

Choose your colors and paper patterns to match the occasion.

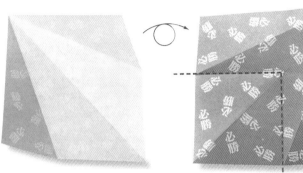

1 First crease a diagonal center line. Crease and return the edges to the center and return.

2 Turn the sheet over. Crease the top left-hand corner from the left edge to the central crease and return. Repeat for the bottom right-hand corner.

3 Raise the lower left-hand corner and bring the sides together. Fold down the sides at an angle, front and back.

4 Tuck both the back and front tips between the layers of paper.

5 This step creates your first module.

6 To join, tuck the flaps at the rear of the right-hand module into the pockets of the left-hand module so that the marked points meet.

7 Fold down the top flap and tuck it inside. The marked points should meet.

8 This picture shows two modules joined together. Join the other modules in the same way.

9 The model must be pulled into three dimensions to make the last join. It can either be concave or convex. The front is convex in this photograph.

10 The back of the napkin ring is seen as concave in this photograph.

simple star

This is an easy model, which consists of four identical modules. They are ideal as decorations or for adding the finishing touch to wrapped presents, particularly if they are made from foil paper.

1 Crease a diagonal centre line. Fold in two corners so that they meet the centre line.

2 This makes the kite base. Now turn the model over.

3 Fold down the top edge so that the top left-hand corner meets the lower corner. The top right-hand corner should lie at the centre line.

4 Mountain-fold the new top left-hand corner behind, then return. This creates your module.

5 To join the modules, tuck the flap of one module inside the pocket of another.

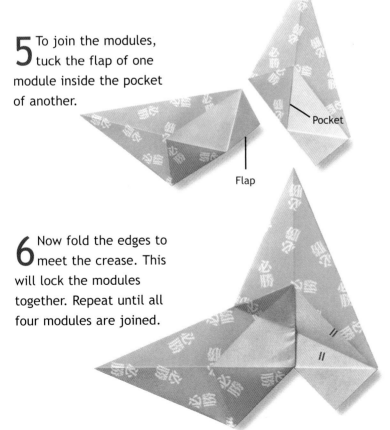

Pocket

Flap

6 Now fold the edges to meet the crease. This will lock the modules together. Repeat until all four modules are joined.

christmas star .... modular designs ◆

This is another festive model that makes an attractive Christmas decoration. It looks particularly nice when it is folded in foil, and there are several variations. You will need four modules with which to make it.

1 First crease a diagonal centre line. Crease and return edges to the centre and return.

2 Turn the sheet over. Crease the top left-hand corner from the left edge to the central crease and return. Repeat for the bottom right-hand corner. Raise the lower left-hand corner and then bring the sides together.

3 Fold down the sides, front and back. The crease runs from point to point.

4 Tuck both the back and front tips between the layers, folding over the layers behind.

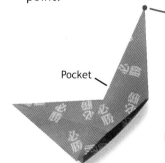

Pocket

Flap

5 Crease the top left-hand corner to the rear and return.

6 To join, tuck the flaps at the rear of the right-hand module into the rear pockets of the left-hand module. The top tip of the left-hand module should meet the tip of the right-hand module.

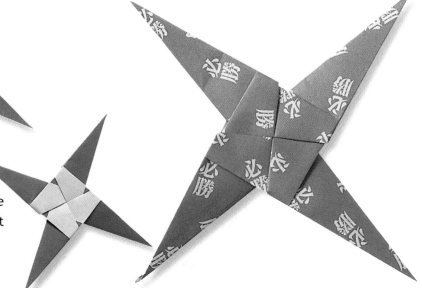

7 This photograph shows two joined modules. Join the remaining units in the same way.

8 Here are some variations that are easily made.

hexagon puzzle

This is a fun puzzle that is surprisingly difficult to solve. We have used practice paper to make the first modules, but you will need to follow the color scheme shown to complete the puzzle. You need six modules for each hexagon.

1 Fold the square in half vertically and return.

2 Take the bottom left-hand corner to a point along the vertical center line just below the top edge (as marked) and return.

3 Now take the top left-hand corner to a point along the center line just above the bottom edge (as marked) and return.

4 Fold in the left-hand edge. Fold from where the two creases meet.

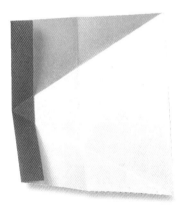

5 Fold down the top right-hand triangle using the existing creases. Fold up the bottom left-hand triangle, again using the existing creases.

6 Fold the bottom right-hand corner to meet the join on the top edge.

7 Tuck the triangle formed at top right inside the layers.

8 This is your first module. You have two pockets at the top.

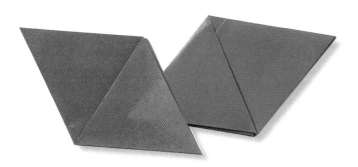

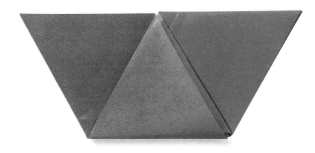

9 To join the modules, slide the point of the right-hand module into the pocket of the left-hand module.

10 This photogrpah shows two modules joined together. Join the others in the same way.

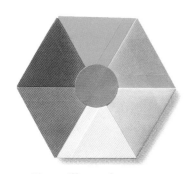

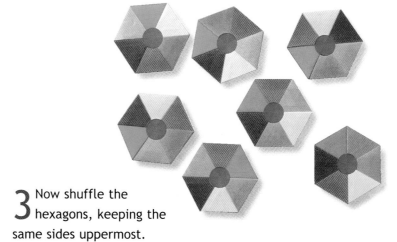

1 You will need seven hexagons for this puzzle. Paint a colored dot on one side of each hexagon, or use a small sticker.

2 Use a different-colored dot or sticker on the other side of each hexagon. If you get the sides confused after the hexagons have been mixed, you will never solve the puzzle!

3 Now shuffle the hexagons, keeping the same sides uppermost.

To complete the puzzle, you need to recreate the pattern shown in the diagram. However, touching colors must be the same. There is only one solution.

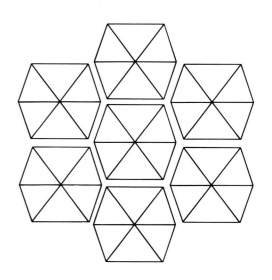

For the solution, see page 128.

millions-to-one wreath

This is a decorative wreath that has a staggering 43,046,721 possible combinations. It would take nearly two years to fold them all – even without allowing time off to eat or sleep! You will need eight modules to create the wreath.

1 First fold a square sheet diagonally in half.

2 Fold the front edge to the bottom edge. Repeat at the rear.

3 Now you need to fold the front flap forward.

4 Fold up the bottom right-hand corner so that it meets a point along the top edge.

5 Crease the flap toward the center line, then open it up again.

6 Now fold the top corner so that it meets a point along the bottom edge.

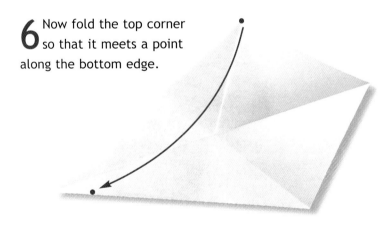

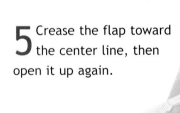

7 Crease the flap toward the center line again and open it out.

8 Make a reverse fold at the right-hand side. Allow the small flaps inside to flip out.

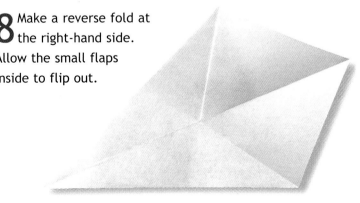

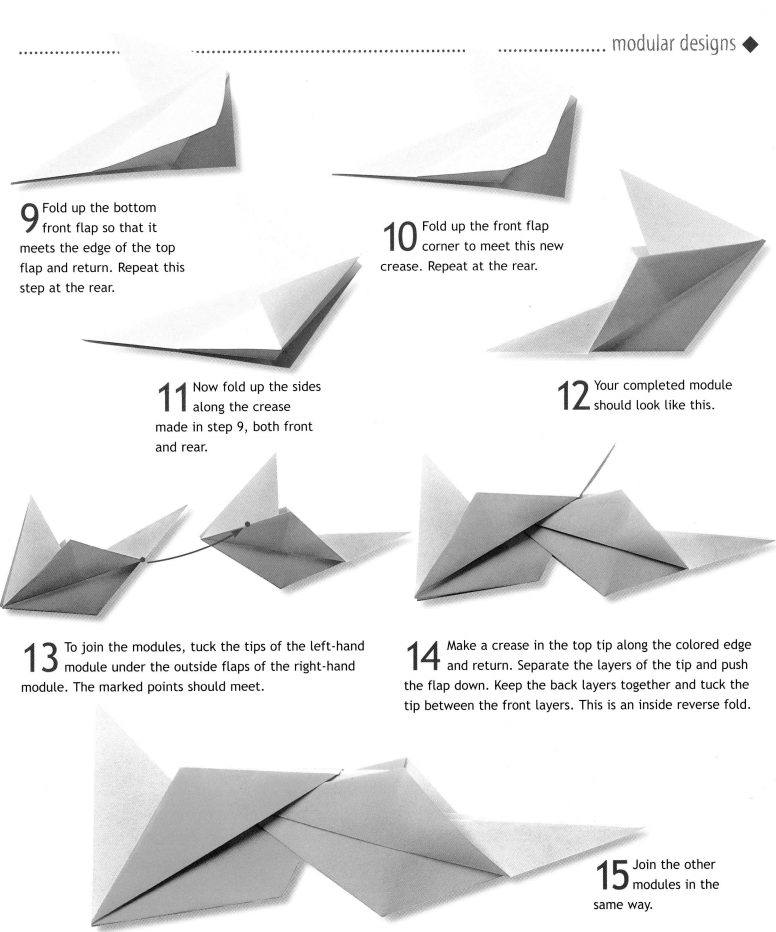

9 Fold up the bottom front flap so that it meets the edge of the top flap and return. Repeat this step at the rear.

10 Fold up the front flap corner to meet this new crease. Repeat at the rear.

11 Now fold up the sides along the crease made in step 9, both front and rear.

12 Your completed module should look like this.

13 To join the modules, tuck the tips of the left-hand module under the outside flaps of the right-hand module. The marked points should meet.

14 Make a crease in the top tip along the colored edge and return. Separate the layers of the tip and push the flap down. Keep the back layers together and tuck the tip between the front layers. This is an inside reverse fold.

15 Join the other modules in the same way.

Here are just three combinations that you can create.

Once you have joined all
of the modules, this is
the result.

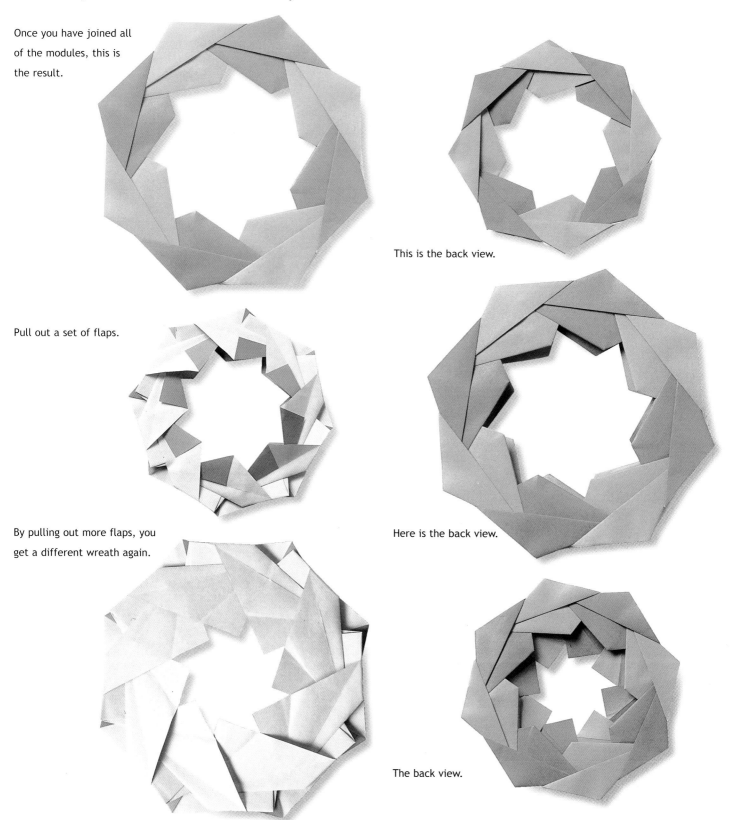

This is the back view.

Pull out a set of flaps.

Here is the back view.

By pulling out more flaps, you
get a different wreath again.

The back view.

christmas wreath

This wreath can be made in different colors to suit different occasions and makes an unusual decoration. You will need to make nine modules.

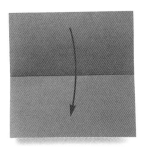   

1 With the colored side face up, fold a square of paper horizontally in half.

2 Fold up the bottom left-hand corner to meet the top right-hand corner and return. Make a reverse fold on the right-hand side.

3 Fold up the front flap to meet the top edge. Repeat at the rear.

4 Tuck the tips, front and back, between the central layers.

5 Now tuck the bottom flaps, both front and back, up between the central layers. The fold should run from corner to corner.

6 This completes your first module. You need nine in total.

7 To join the modules, tuck the bottom tips of the right-hand module between the layers at the front of the left-hand unit.

 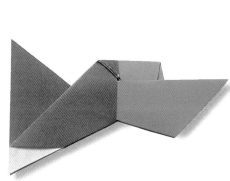 

8 Tuck the top tip of the two joined units between the lower layers. The point where the white and the colored paper join at the top edge should meet the corner of the top edge of the pocket.

9 This shows two modules joined correctly. Add the next module to the right-hand side and continue in the same way for the other modules.

flower wheel .... modular designs ◆

This is a pretty example of the wheel pattern, which can be made using any mix of colors. However, the pattern of the paper is so delicate that it can be very effective in one color. You will need 13 modules.

1 Take one edge of the paper to meet the opposite edge. Do not fold, only make a pinch.

2 Now fold the paper in half diagonally.

3 Fold the left-hand corner to meet the pinch on the right-hand edge. Now return. Make the creases into a reverse fold.

4 Now down fold the flaps, front and rear.

5 Tuck in the rear tips between the layers, folding them over the layer behind them.

6 This picture shows the completed module.

7 To join the modules, tuck the tips of the right-hand module into the pockets either side of the left-hand module. The marked points should meet.

8 Fold the tip on the outside, lining up the marked points, then tuck the folded part between the layers.

9 This photograph shows two joined modules. Continue adding modules to the right.

the big wheel

There are a variety of different wheels that you can make, each using slightly different modules. Here we will look at two examples of wheels. Again, the colours can be combined in any way you wish.

wheel 1 ◆ Use 7cm paper to give you a 25cm diameter wheel. You will need 24 modules.

1 With the coloured side face up, take one edge of the paper to meet the opposite edge. Do not fold, only make a pinch.

2 Now fold the paper in half diagonally.

3 Fold the left-hand corner to meet the pinch on the right-hand edge. Now return. Make a reverse fold at the left-hand corner.

4 Now fold down the flaps, front and rear.

5 Tuck in the rear tips between the layers.

6 This is the completed module. It is the same as the module for the flower wheel on page 75, but the assembly of the wheel is different.

7 Tuck the tips of the right-hand module into the pockets of the left-hand module. The points marked on the photographs should meet.

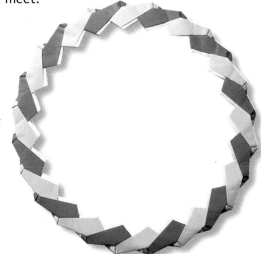

8 Tuck the tip into the pocket. The marked points should meet.

9 Here are two joined modules. Join the others from the right.

wheel 2 ◆ Use 7cm paper to give you a 22cm diameter wheel. You will need 22 modules.

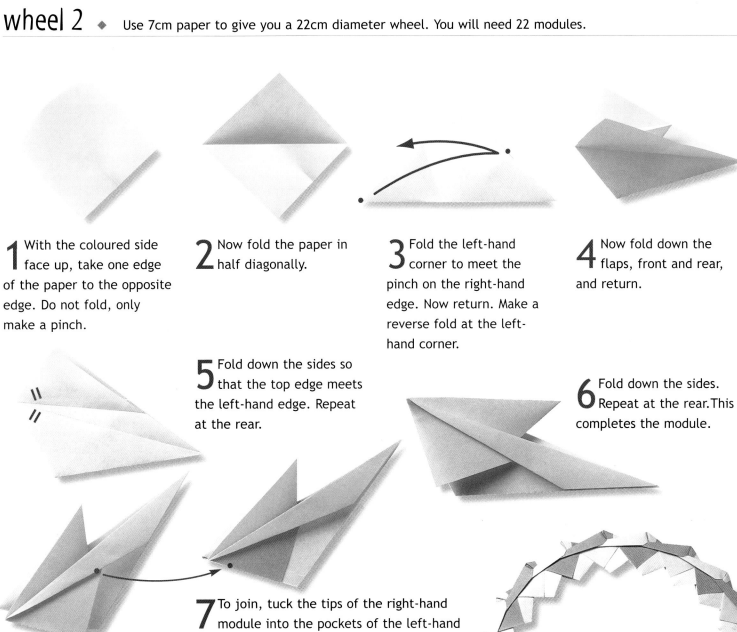

1 With the coloured side face up, take one edge of the paper to the opposite edge. Do not fold, only make a pinch.

2 Now fold the paper in half diagonally.

3 Fold the left-hand corner to meet the pinch on the right-hand edge. Now return. Make a reverse fold at the left-hand corner.

4 Now fold down the flaps, front and rear, and return.

5 Fold down the sides so that the top edge meets the left-hand edge. Repeat at the rear.

6 Fold down the sides. Repeat at the rear. This completes the module.

7 To join, tuck the tips of the right-hand module into the pockets of the left-hand module. The marked points should meet.

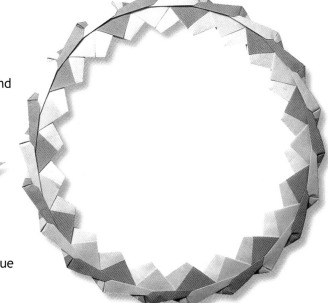

8 Tuck the middle tip into the pocket.

9 This shows two joined modules. Continue adding modules from the right.

stumpy star

This model is so called because instead of points the arms of the star are blunted. Both sides of the star are equally decorative. To make the star you will need to make five star modules.

1 With the coloured side face up, fold the paper in half diagonally.

2 Fold front flap diagonally to meet the bottom edge. Repeat at rear.

3 Fold the front flap forward.

4 Take the bottom corner to meet the top edge as marked above.

5 Crease flap to the centre line, and then open it up.

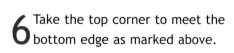

6 Take the top corner to meet the bottom edge as marked above.

7 Crease the flap to the centre line and open up.

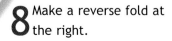

8 Make a reverse fold at the right.

9 Tuck the right-hand tips between the layers.

10 Here is the completed module.

11 Prepare the modules by folding the flaps to the centre, front and back.

12 To join the modules, tuck the flaps of the left-hand module inside the right-hand module. The marked points should meet.

13 Now tuck the middle tip between the layers to lock.

14 This shows two joined modules. Add further modules from the left.

15 The model has to be pulled into three dimensions to complete the joining of the final module. This picture shows the locks on the inside.

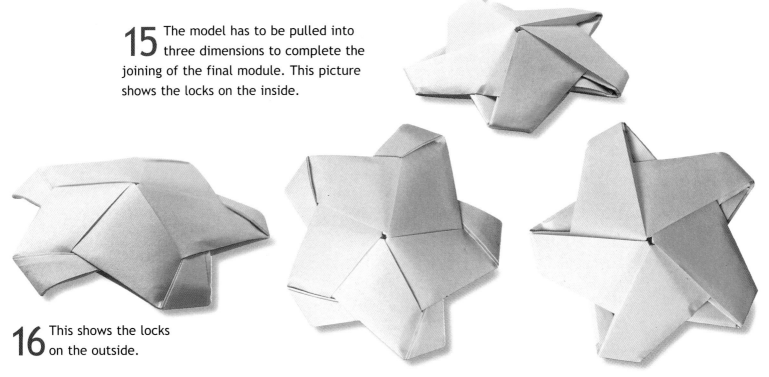

16 This shows the locks on the outside.

decorated stumpy star ....

This also uses the stumpy-star modules as a base, but adds some folds to create a more decorative finish. You will need five modules. Follow steps 1 to 8 for the stumpy-star before continuing as instructed below.

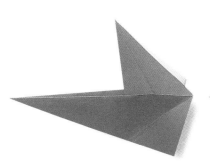

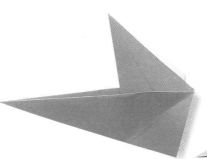

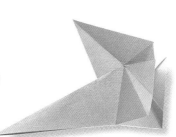

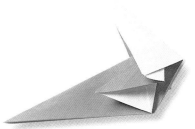

1 Fold and return both the front and rear flaps.

2 Fold and return the right-hand edges, both front and rear.

3 Fold up the bottom corner, then fold down the top flap. Repeat at rear.

4 Your completed module should look like this.

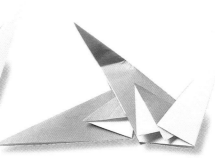

5 To join the modules, tuck the flaps of the left-hand module inside the right-hand module. The marked points should meet.

6 Now tuck the middle tip between the layers.

7 Here are two joined modules. Add further modules from the left.

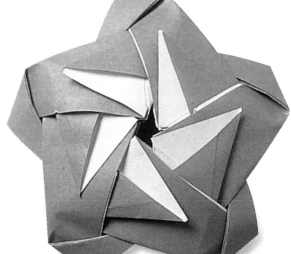

8 The model has to be pulled into three dimensions to complete the joining of the last module.

borealis .... modular designs ◆

This is a complex modular design, and using bright colors makes it a very beautiful model. You first need to create 30 modules.

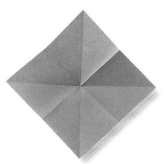

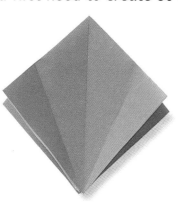

1 Form a preliminary base (see page 14), with the colored side outward.

2 Fold the edges of the front flaps to the center and return. Repeat at rear.

3 Sink the top point. The crease joins the end of the crease made in step 2.

4 Swivel the right-hand flap to the left.

5 This picture shows the completed module.

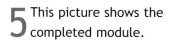

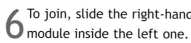

7 Fold the tip at right angles to lock it.

6 To join, slide the right-hand module inside the left one.

8 This photograph shows two joined modules.

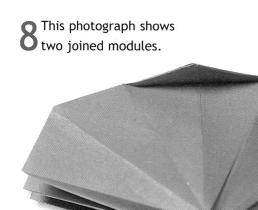

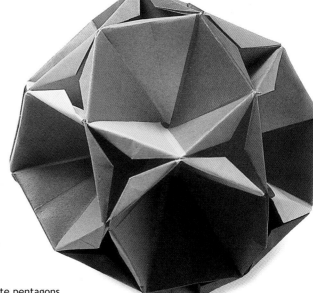

Thirty modules combined create pentagons with triangles on each side.

81 ◆

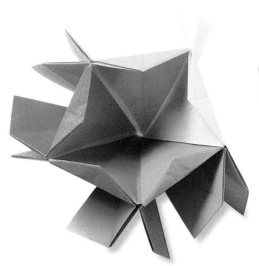

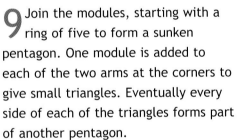

9 Join the modules, starting with a ring of five to form a sunken pentagon. One module is added to each of the two arms at the corners to give small triangles. Eventually every side of each of the triangles forms part of another pentagon.

10 This photograph shows six units joined – a pentagon with a triangle on one corner.

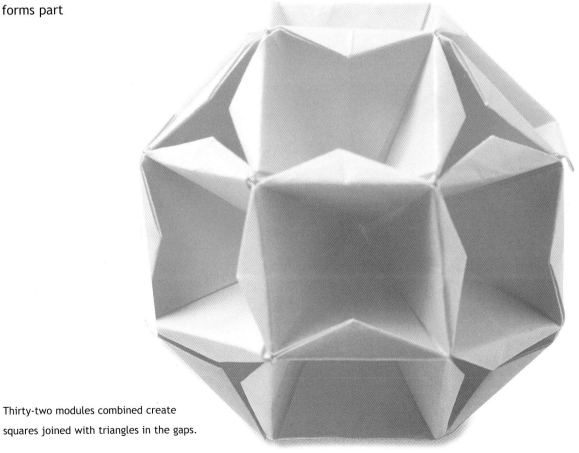

Thirty-two modules combined create squares joined with triangles in the gaps.

Other shapes can be made
using the same modules.

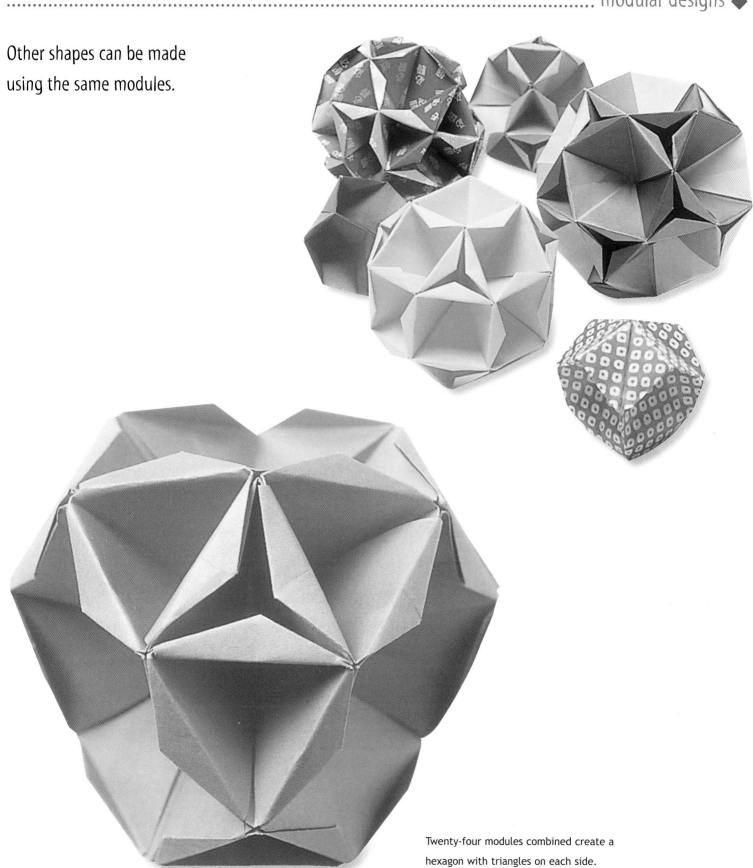

Twenty-four modules combined create a
hexagon with triangles on each side.

6 animals and plants

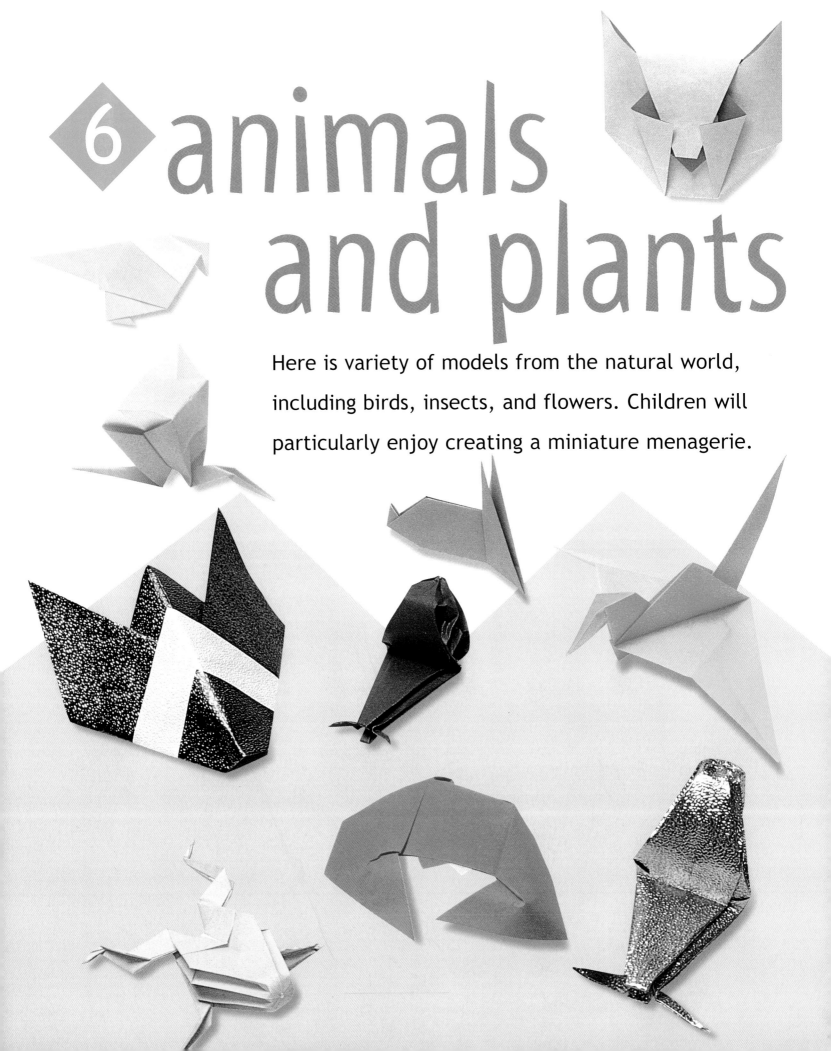

Here is variety of models from the natural world, including birds, insects, and flowers. Children will particularly enjoy creating a miniature menagerie.

baby rabbit .... animals and plants ◆

A cute model that will probably work best with larger paper, as it involves hidden folds that can be tricky to manipulate at a very small scale. It begins with a square, white side face up.

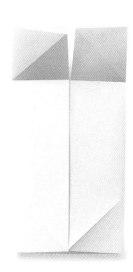

1 Crease both diagonals and then a vertical center line. Fold both sides to the center.

2 Now fold the top edge to the center.

3 Carefully pull out the hidden corners on both sides. Using mountain folds, fold the two top and two bottom corners to the rear.

4 Fold the model in half, using a mountain fold.

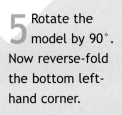

5 Rotate the model by 90°. Now reverse-fold the bottom left-hand corner.

6 Fold the head at an angle to make the rabbit stand upright.

fat rabbit

A fun model that requires inflating to complete. It begins with a waterbomb base, made with the colored side of the paper face up.

1 Form the waterbomb base (see page 15 for full instructions).

3 Now fold the upper top corners into the middle.

2 Fold up the bottom corners of the bottom layer to meet the top corner.

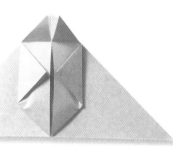

4 Fold down the upper edges of the top layer to meet the folded edges.

5 Tuck the flaps inside the pockets formed by previous folds.

7 Once you have neatly tucked away the flaps, turn the model over.

6 Tuck the flaps in carefully, avoiding creating wrinkles.

8 Fold the two bottom corners up to the top corner.

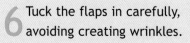

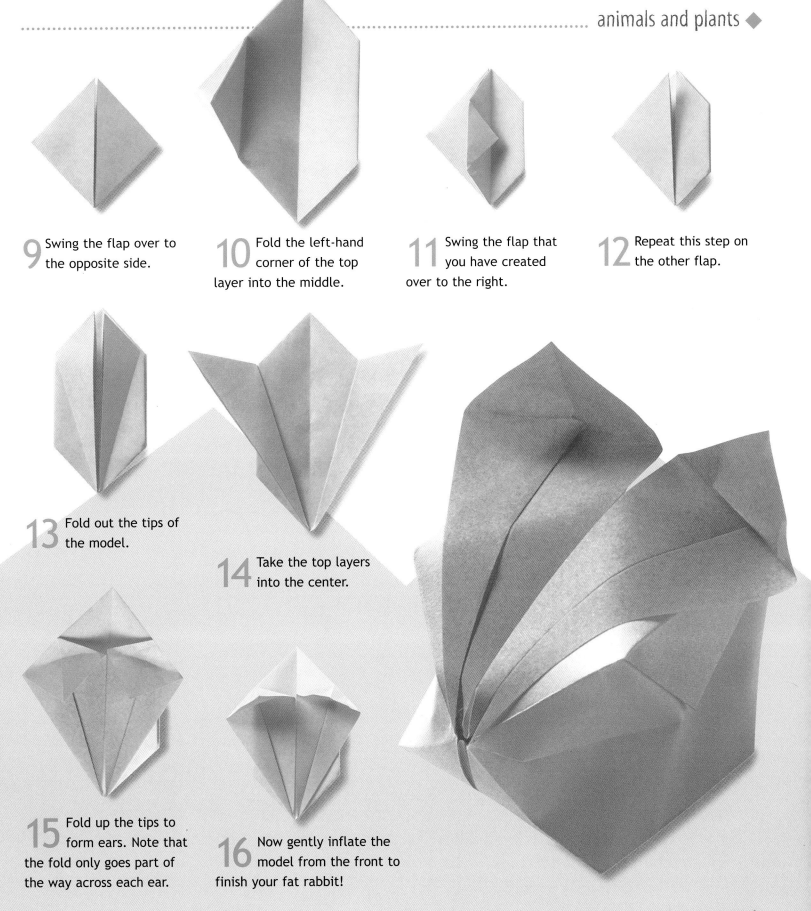

9 Swing the flap over to the opposite side.

10 Fold the left-hand corner of the top layer into the middle.

11 Swing the flap that you have created over to the right.

12 Repeat this step on the other flap.

13 Fold out the tips of the model.

14 Take the top layers into the center.

15 Fold up the tips to form ears. Note that the fold only goes part of the way across each ear.

16 Now gently inflate the model from the front to finish your fat rabbit!

caterpillar

An entertaining model made in three parts – it can be as long as you like. The modules for the body should be made first. Each part requires the same-sized square paper.

body

1 With the white side face up, fold the paper diagonally in half.

2 Fold the left-hand tip of the front layer to meet the right-hand edge.

3 Valley-fold the model in half from top to bottom. This creates your first body segment. Make several of these.

4 To join the body segments, insert the top right-hand corner of one segment over the inside flap of the second segment. Continue until you have as many segments as you wish.

neck

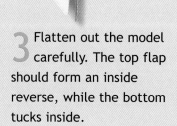

1 Begin with a square with both center lines creased from corner to corner. Valley-fold the left- and right-hand corners to the center. Mountain-fold the bottom corner to the rear, also to the center.

2 Mountain-fold the model in half vertically and return. Make valley folds as indicated. Pull the top and bottom together using the creases you have made.

3 Flatten out the model carefully. The top flap should form an inside reverse, while the bottom tucks inside.

4 To connect the neck to the body, slide it over the top right-hand corner of the first segment.

head

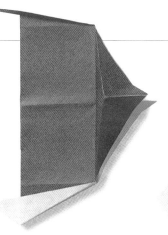

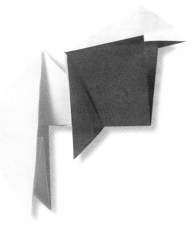

1 Begin with a square with both center lines creased from corner to corner. Fold each corner to the center and return.

2 Make mountain folds in both the top and bottom flap, as indicated. Valley-fold the model in half vertically. This creates outside reverse folds at the top and bottom.

3 Now make mountain folds on the right-hand flap, as indicated. Then mountain-fold the model horizontally, working from front to back.

4 This creates the head. Slide it onto the neck to finish your caterpillar.

bird

This amusing three-dimensional model is simple to fold. The inside reverse fold is quite small, so care needs to be taken not to crumple the paper.

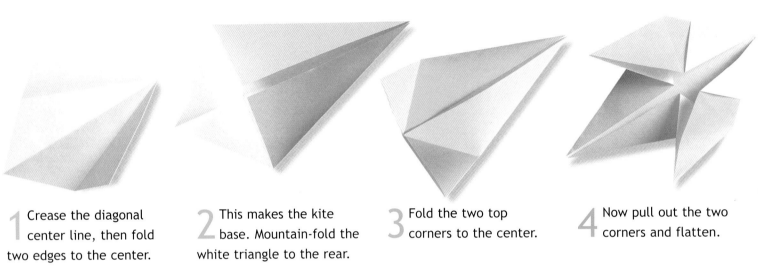

1 Crease the diagonal center line, then fold two edges to the center.

2 This makes the kite base. Mountain-fold the white triangle to the rear.

3 Fold the two top corners to the center.

4 Now pull out the two corners and flatten.

5 Form the bird's feet by folding up the tips of both flaps. Now valley-fold the model in half.

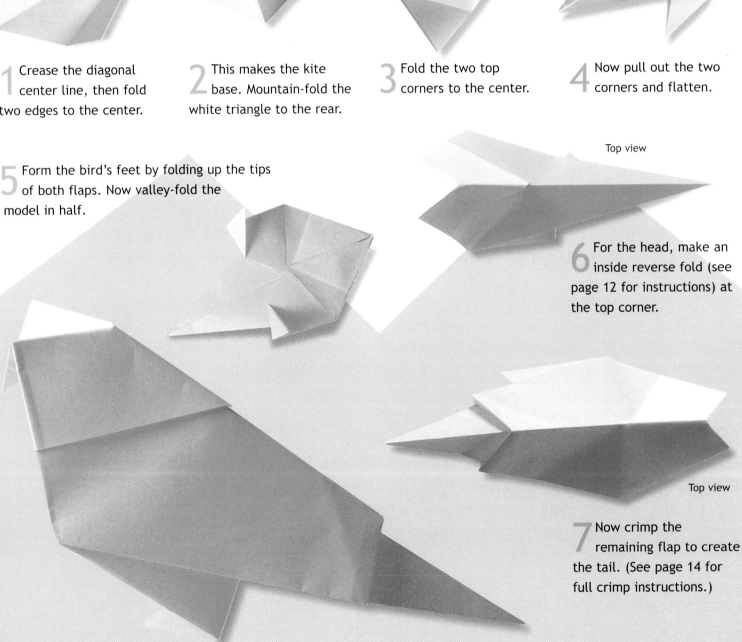

Top view

6 For the head, make an inside reverse fold (see page 12 for instructions) at the top corner.

Top view

7 Now crimp the remaining flap to create the tail. (See page 14 for full crimp instructions.)

grasshopper .... animals and plants ◆

Also known as the cicada. This very simple, three-dimensional model makes excellent use of both sides of the paper. It can be very effective when made with glittering foil.

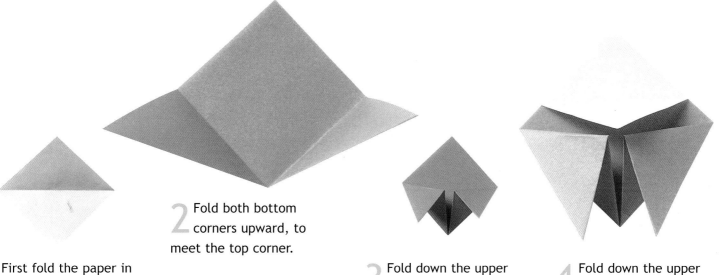

2 Fold both bottom corners upward, to meet the top corner.

1 First fold the paper in half diagonally.

3 Fold down the upper tips of the top layer at a slight angle.

4 Fold down the upper flap of the top layer.

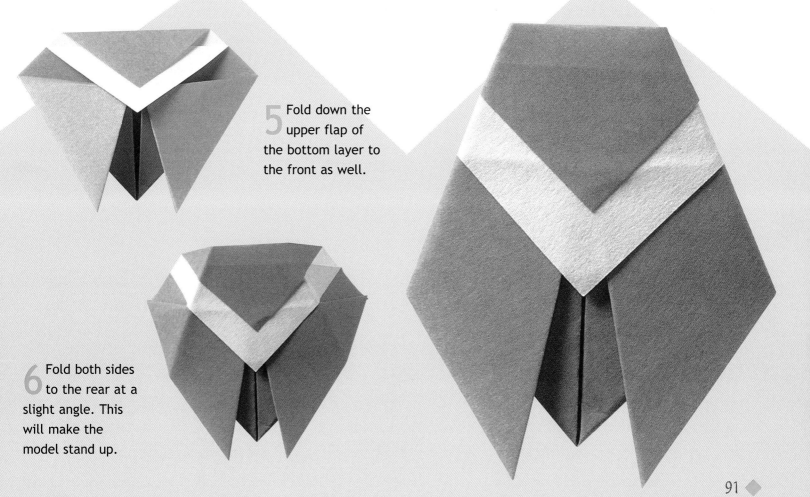

5 Fold down the upper flap of the bottom layer to the front as well.

6 Fold both sides to the rear at a slight angle. This will make the model stand up.

91 ◆

butterfly

This is a very pretty model, which is particularly effective when made with foil or colored origami paper.

1 Fold and return both diagonal creases.

2 Fold each of the four corners into the center.

3 This creates a blintz base. Turn this over.

4 Fold and return each of the corners to the center.

5 Turn the model over again and open out the four corners.

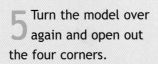

6 Fold the top and bottom edges into the center.

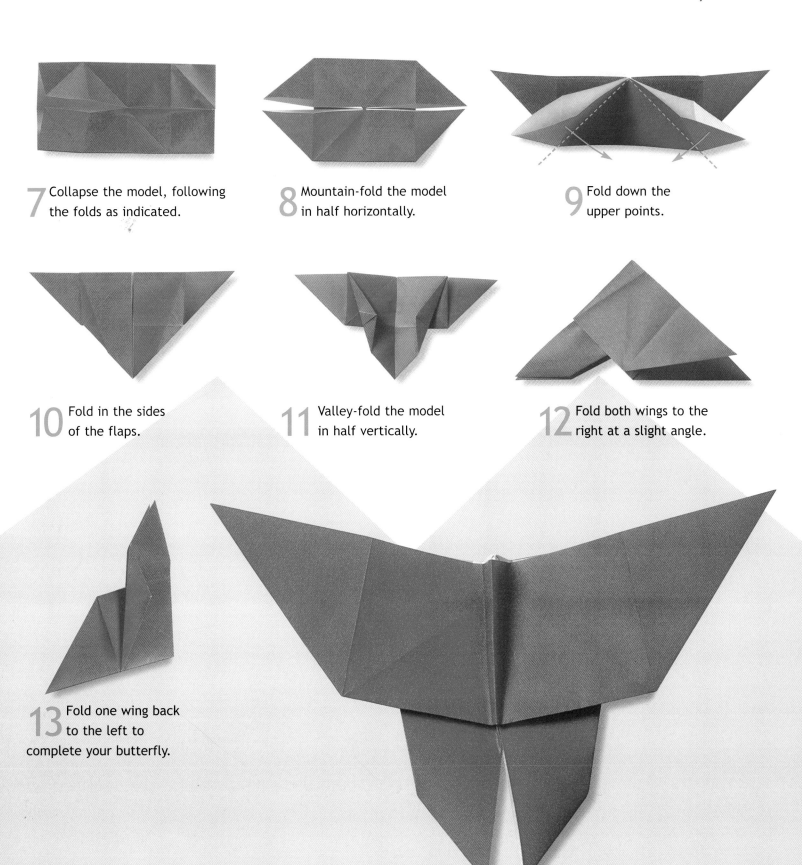

7 Collapse the model, following the folds as indicated.

8 Mountain-fold the model in half horizontally.

9 Fold down the upper points.

10 Fold in the sides of the flaps.

11 Valley-fold the model in half vertically.

12 Fold both wings to the right at a slight angle.

13 Fold one wing back to the left to complete your butterfly.

pajarita

This is a traditional European model (pajarita means "little bird" in Spanish). It is known as the "rooster" in the U.S.A. The flapping action is attributed to Kuni Kasahara.

1 Crease and return the horizontal and vertical center lines.

2 Then crease and return the diagonal center lines.

3 Fold the four corners into the center to form a blintz.

4 Now mountain-fold the four corners to the rear to make a further blintz.

5 Next open out the folded paper fully.

6 To fold the model, first fold along the diagonal of the center square. The rest of the folds should follow automatically.

7 This forms your pajarita shape. Either hold it at the points marked or pull and return to flap the wings.

mandarin duck .... animals and plants ◆

This attractive three-dimensional model may require some practice as it involves several reverse folds. You may find this easier to do with a large sheet of paper.

 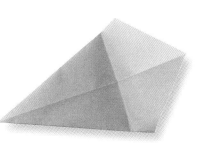  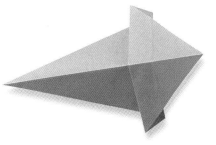

1 First crease a diagonal center line. Then fold two edges to this center line to form a kite base.

2 Turn the paper over. Fold in the tip. The corners should not meet.

3 Now fold the white triangle outward, to the right.

4 Next mountain-fold the model horizontally in half.

 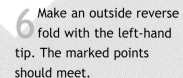

5 Fold up the bottom flap so that the bottom right-hand corner meets the top edge as marked. Repeat at the rear.

6 Make an outside reverse fold with the left-hand tip. The marked points should meet.

7 Next make a further outside reverse fold with this top tip.

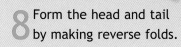

8 Form the head and tail by making reverse folds.

cat face

A series of folds makes up this amusing model. Try experimenting with different folds to see if you can create other animal faces.

1 Crease and return both diagonals. Then fold and return two edges to one of the diagonal creases.

2 Fold and return the top corner. The crease should join the ends of the existing creases.

3 Fold the bottom corner so that it meets the point where the diagonal centre line and the new crease join. Then return.

4 Fold the bottom corner to meet the point where the new crease joins the diagonal centre line.

5 Pleat the bottom triangle. Fold the bottom part to the rear, then turn the paper over.

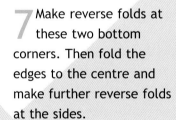

6 Fold and return the bottom corners. Each fold should pass through he intersection of the existing creases.

7 Make reverse folds at these two bottom corners. Then fold the edges to the centre and make further reverse folds at the sides.

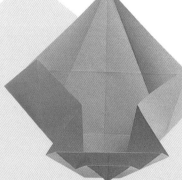

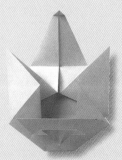

8 Blunt the sharp point at the top, then fold this tip down and tuck it in behind the bottom pleat.

9 Valley-fold the front flaps and tuck them under the central flap.

plump crane

animals and plants ◆

This three-dimensional model is a quite straightforward version of the traditional crane.
Care must be taken when forming the tail and beak as they are prone to crumpling.

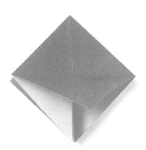

1 First form a preliminary base, as demonstrated on page 14.

2 Fold up the bottom flap of the front layer to the top corner. Repeat the process on the rear flap.

3 Fold the left- and right-hand corners of the front layer to the center. Repeat at the rear.

4 Now fold the sides, both the front and the back, into the center.

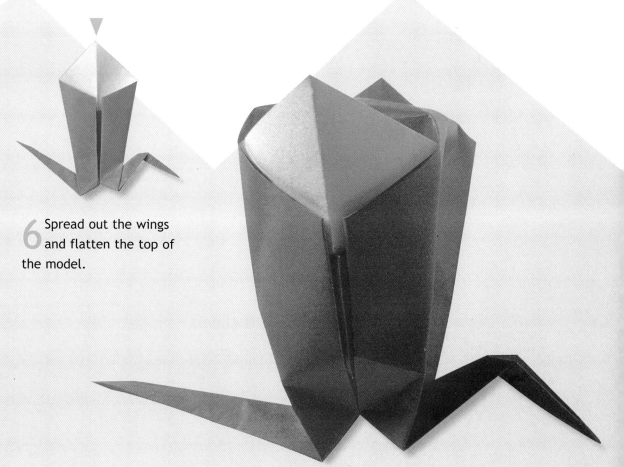

6 Spread out the wings and flatten the top of the model.

5 Reverse-fold the front and rear. Make an additional reverse fold near the tip of one of the long points to make the beak.

winking crab

A variation of an original model, using paper of different colors on each side to create the winking effect. For a uniform crab, use paper of the same color on both sides.

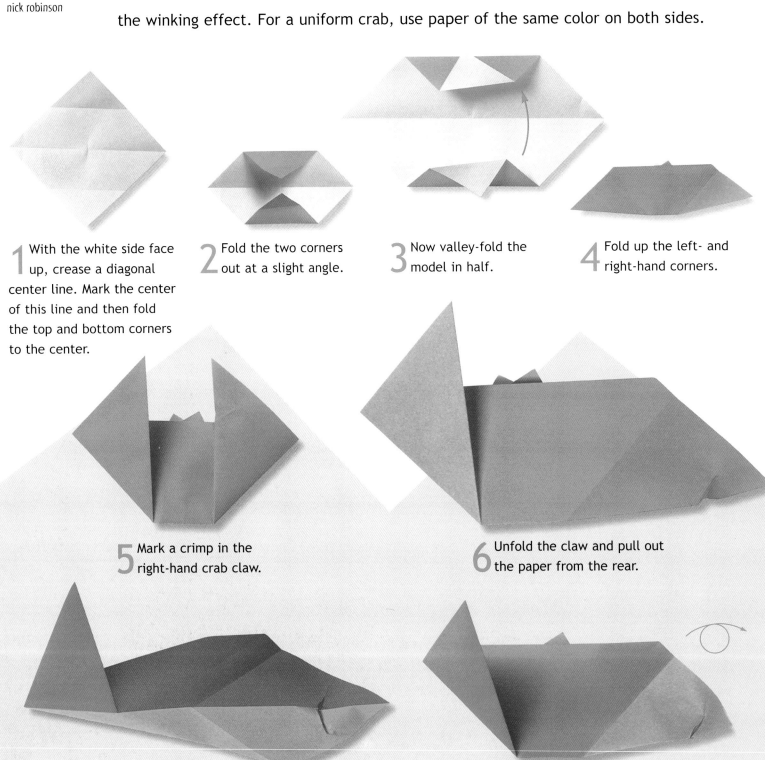

1 With the white side face up, crease a diagonal center line. Mark the center of this line and then fold the top and bottom corners to the center.

2 Fold the two corners out at a slight angle.

3 Now valley-fold the model in half.

4 Fold up the left- and right-hand corners.

5 Mark a crimp in the right-hand crab claw.

6 Unfold the claw and pull out the paper from the rear.

7 Turn the model upside down to complete the crimp and return flap.

8 Fold the flap back up to the top.

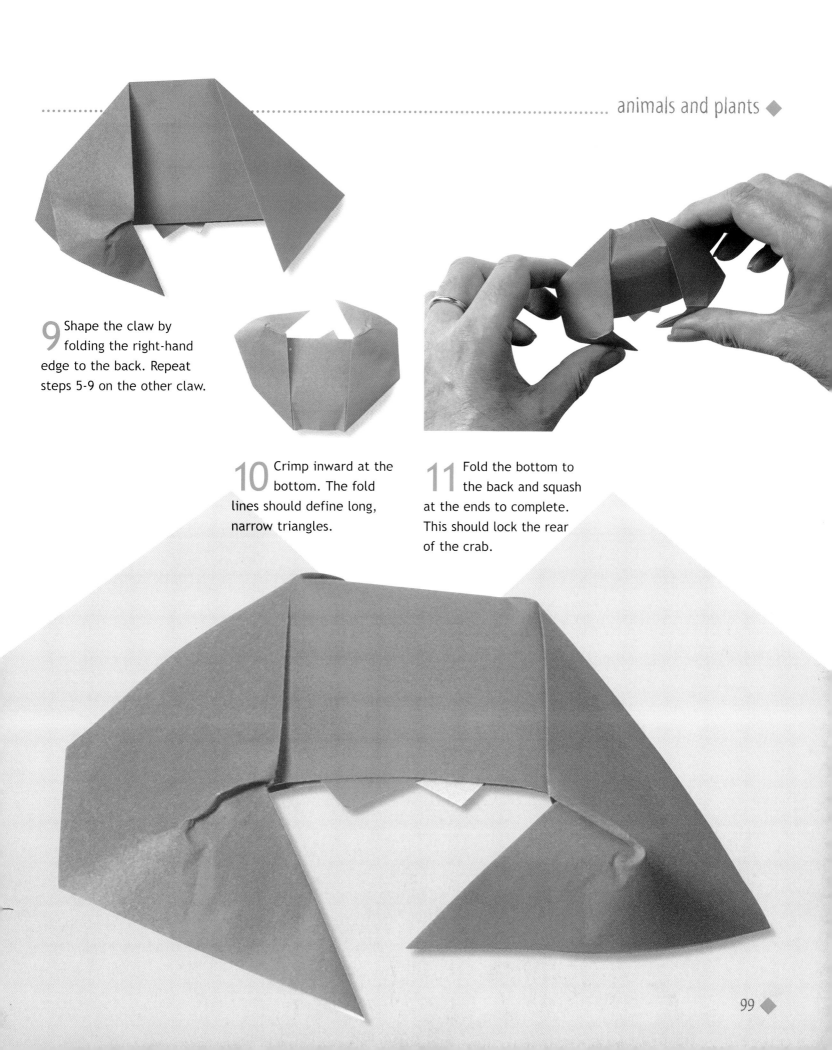

9 Shape the claw by folding the right-hand edge to the back. Repeat steps 5-9 on the other claw.

10 Crimp inward at the bottom. The fold lines should define long, narrow triangles.

11 Fold the bottom to the back and squash at the ends to complete. This should lock the rear of the crab.

flapping bird ....

This is the best-known of all the traditional models, and is a fun, moving model to create. It begins with the bird base (see page 16).

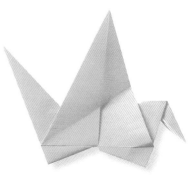

1 Make an inside reverse fold at the right-hand corner. Make a further inside reverse fold at the tip of the flap that you have just created.

2 Make another inside reverse fold at the left-hand corner.

3 Fold the bottom flaps, front and rear layers, to the top to form the wings.

4 Valley-fold the back edge of the front wing down to the horizontal. Repeat at the rear.

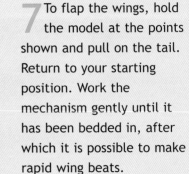

5 Now gently spread out the wings.

6 Press at the back of the wing to break the ridge. Repeat at the rear.

7 To flap the wings, hold the model at the points shown and pull on the tail. Return to your starting position. Work the mechanism gently until it has been bedded in, after which it is possible to make rapid wing beats.

fall leaf

difficulty :

origin :
david petty

A group of these leaves can make a very pretty display, and the fall leaf is quite easy to fold. It begins with a square with both diagonal creases folded and returned.

1 Fold two of the edges to one of the center diagonal creases.

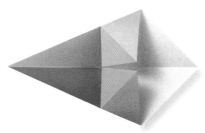

2 Valley-fold the model in half horizontally.

3 Fold back the front tip at the halfway point on the lower colored layer.

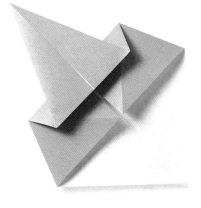

4 Pull out both lower flaps from under the central layers.

5 Reverse-fold both side flaps. Fold the top tip inward to blunt the tip.

6 Narrow the stalk by folding the sides to the center. Squash at the bottom corners (see page 12 for squash instructions).

7 Fold the stalk at an angle and blunt the corners of the main part of the leaf. Turn over. To make the leaf stand up, fold and return both top corners.

frog

This fun three-dimensional model needs care and attention to avoid crumpling. The model will require inflating at the end. It begins with a frog base (see page 18).

1 Bring the left-hand front flap to the right. Repeat the process at the rear. This is a book fold.

2 Fold the lower edges to the center line. Repeat at the rear.

3 Book-fold the model once more, as in step 1.

4 Fold the lower edges to the center line. Repeat at the rear.

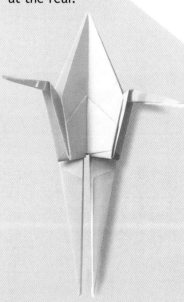

5 Now make a further book fold.

6 Make inside reverse folds on the upper layers as far up as the paper will allow. The outer edge should lie on the existing edge.

7 Make inside reverse folds on the flaps that you have just created, left and right.

8 This picture shows how the model should look at this stage.

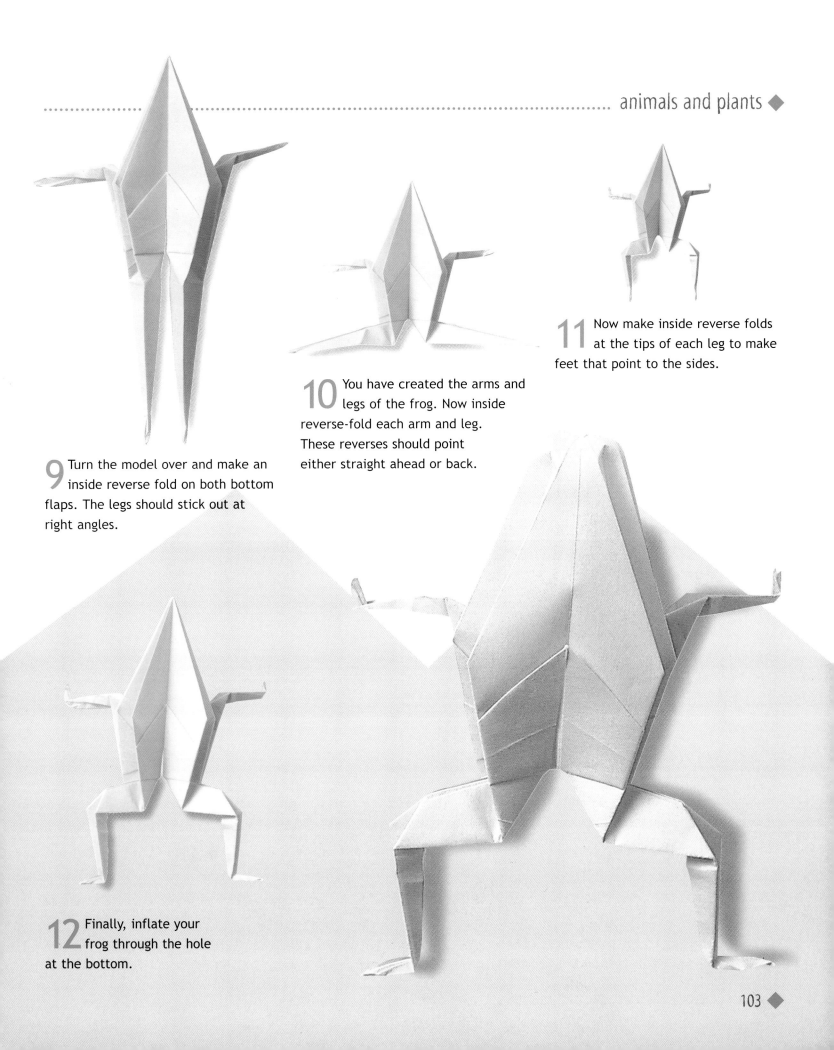

11 Now make inside reverse folds at the tips of each leg to make feet that point to the sides.

10 You have created the arms and legs of the frog. Now inside reverse-fold each arm and leg. These reverses should point either straight ahead or back.

9 Turn the model over and make an inside reverse fold on both bottom flaps. The legs should stick out at right angles.

12 Finally, inflate your frog through the hole at the bottom.

snail

This three-dimensional model is one of the most difficult to complete successfully. It also requires care to avoid crumpling. Practice several times on scrap paper before using proper origami paper.

1 With the white side face up, first form a preliminary base (page 14).

2 Squash the right-hand flap at the front and also at the back.

3 Bring the right-hand flap over to the left for a book fold. Repeat at rear.

4 Squash the remaining right-hand flap. Repeat at the process at the rear.

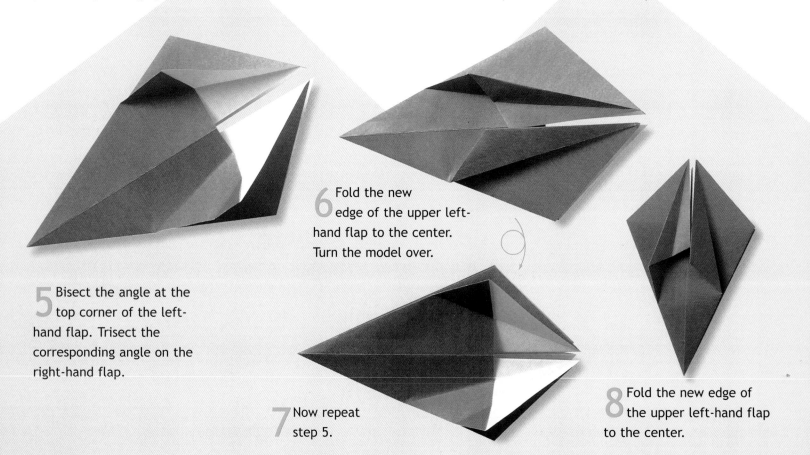

5 Bisect the angle at the top corner of the left-hand flap. Trisect the corresponding angle on the right-hand flap.

6 Fold the new edge of the upper left-hand flap to the center. Turn the model over.

7 Now repeat step 5.

8 Fold the new edge of the upper left-hand flap to the center.

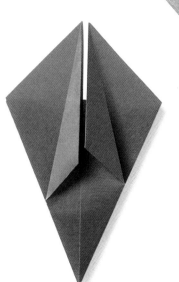

10 Bisect the angle at the top corner of the left-hand flap. Trisect the corresponding angle on the right-hand flap. Now repeat at the rear.

9 Book-fold the left-hand flap to the right and repeat at the rear.

11 Next fold the flaps at both the front and the back.

12 Book-fold the right-hand flap to the left and repeat at the rear.

13 Reverse-fold the left- and right-hand tips to form the snail's horns.

14 Tuck the tip of the front flap between the layers of paper.

15 Tuck the tip of the rear flap between the layers of paper.

16 Adjust the angle of the horns by raising them slightly.

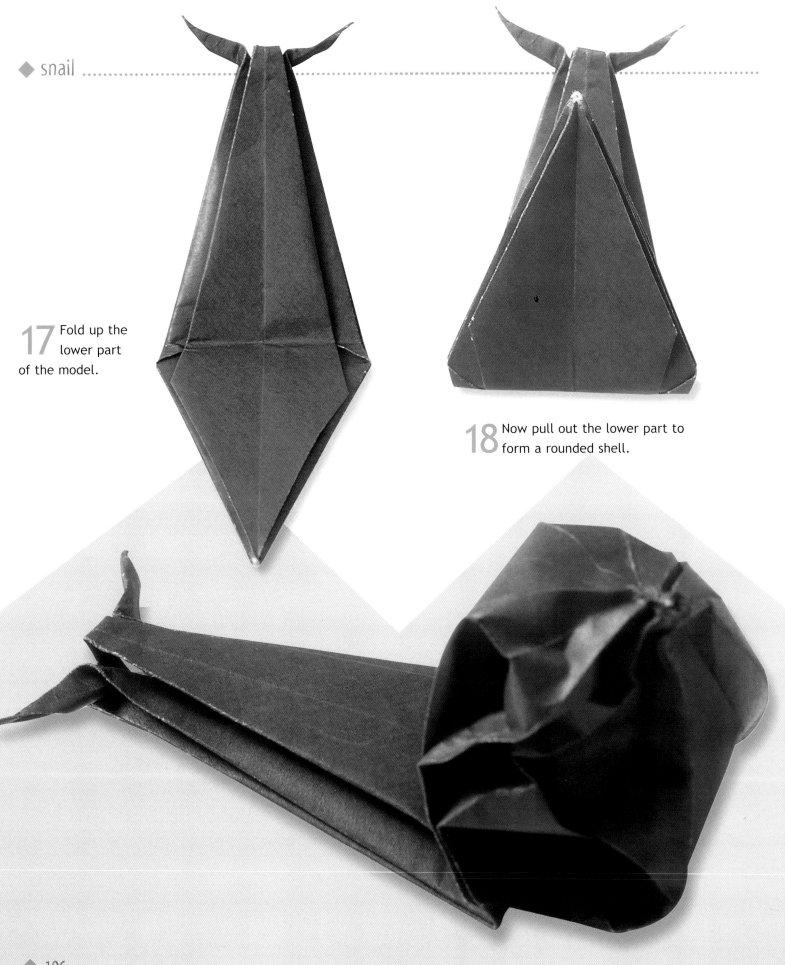

17 Fold up the lower part of the model.

18 Now pull out the lower part to form a rounded shell.

fuchsia

.... animals and plants ◆

As with the fall leaf, these models form a lovely display if you group several of them together. Because you will need to make a number of complex folds, try working with larger paper first.

1 With the paper's white side face up, form a preliminary base (page 14).

2 Squash-fold each of the flaps in turn.

3 Fold in the edges by about one-third, then return. Repeat on all flaps. Open out the paper.

4 Pleat one section of the sheet along the existing crease lines.

5 The model is now three-dimensional. Valley-fold the top layer and squash the lower layer.

6 Repeat step 5 on all four sides.

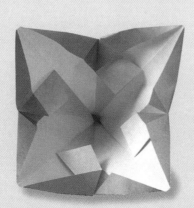

7 This shows an inside view of the fuchsia.

⬥7 transport

A selection of cars, boats, trains, and a plane. Many of these models are quick and easy to make, although the 3D models require more patience and practice.

jet plane

.... transport ◆

Although this is an easy model to fold, you need to make the creases and angles accurate, otherwise your jet will not fly.

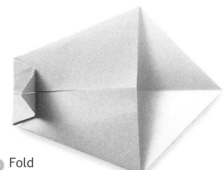

1 Crease a central diagonal line. Now fold two of the edges to this center line.

2 This gives you a kite base. Valley-fold the tip about one-quarter of the way along the diagonal.

3 Fold this tip back, leaving a pleat.

Upside down

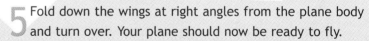

4 Valley-fold the model in half.

5 Fold down the wings at right angles from the plane body and turn over. Your plane should now be ready to fly.

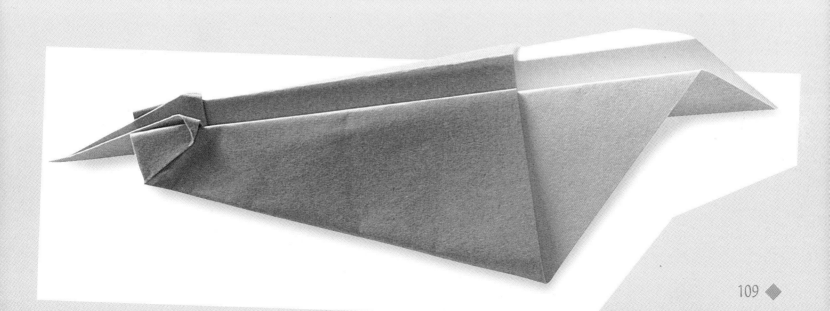

train set

The next projects allow you to create an entire train set, comprising a locomotive, a passenger coach, an open freight car, and a closed freight car. You can make as many of the last three models as you wish. This folding routine is the basis for several transport models and can easily be adapted to make vehicles of your own.

locomotive

1 Crease the center line vertically. Fold the paper horizontally, but do not crease it. Now make a small pinch at the center.

2 Fold the bottom edge to meet this pinch at the center.

3 Fold down the corners of this bottom flap. Note that the folds do not go all the way into the corners.

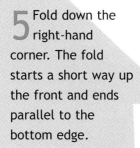

5 Fold down the right-hand corner. The fold starts a short way up the front and ends parallel to the bottom edge.

4 Blunt these bottom corners by folding the very tips up. Turn the model over.

6 Mountain-fold the top part to the rear to complete your locomotive.

passenger coach

1 Crease the center line vertically. Fold the paper horizontally, but do not crease. Make a small pinch at the center.

2 Fold the bottom edge to meet this pinch at the center.

3 Fold down the corners of this bottom flap. Note that the folds do not go all the way into the corners.

4 Blunt these bottom corners by folding the very tips up. Turn the model over.

5 Fold down the top edge. This fold should leave a colored strip below when complete. Fold the top corners to the rear to finish.

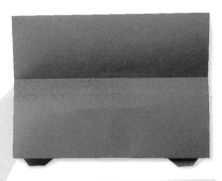

open freight car

1 Crease the center line vertically. Fold the paper horizontally, but do not crease it. Now make a small pinch at the center.

2 Fold the bottom edge to meet this pinch at the center.

3 Fold down the corners of this bottom flap. Note that the folds do not go all the way into the corners.

4 Blunt these bottom corners by folding the very tips up. Fold down the top edge.

5 Fold the two bottom corners to the center crease.

6 Fold the bottom tip up to the top edge, then turn over to finish.

closed freight car

1 Crease the center line vertically. Fold the paper horizontally, but do not crease it. Now make a small pinch at the center.

2 Fold the bottom edge to meet this pinch at the center.

3 Fold down the corners of this bottom flap. Note that the folds do not go all the way into the corners.

4 Blunt these bottom corners by folding the very tips up. Fold down the top edge to touch the center point.

5 Next fold up the bottom edge of the top flap.

6 Inside reverse both top corners (see page 12 for full instructions).

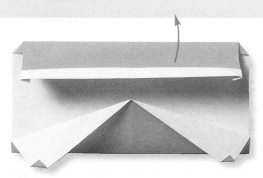

7 Fold the ends of the top band inside. Fold up the flap and turn the model over to finish.

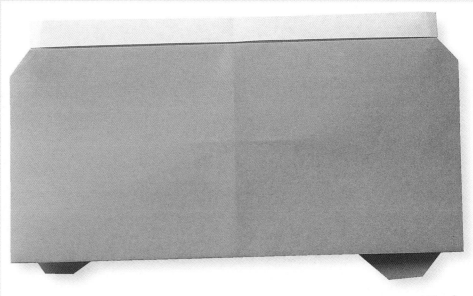

yacht

A number of small folds are needed for this model, so it is probably better to use a large-sized paper. This model begins with the paper colored side face up.

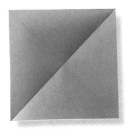

1 First crease both diagonal center lines and then return.

2 Fold the left-hand and top edges to meet the diagonal crease and then return.

3 Fold the top left-hand corner from where the two creases meet. The tip of the corner should lie on the diagonal crease.

4 Fold back the tip, making the fold along the line that has been formed between the ends of the existing creases.

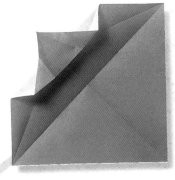

5 Mountain-fold the edges of the triangle to the rear.

6 Fold down both corners on either side of the triangle, working along the existing creases.

7 Fold up the right-hand and bottom edges to make the yacht's hull. This can be as deep as you wish. Now reverse-fold the model.

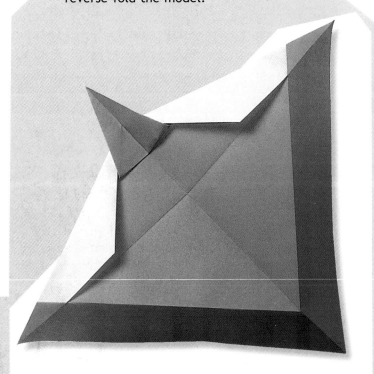

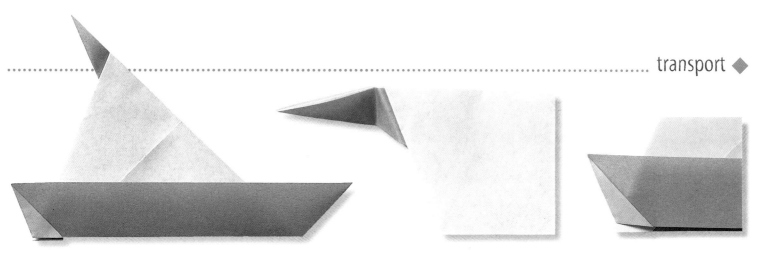

8 This gives you your basic yacht shape.

9 Now crimp the flag inside, so that it points to the side.

10 Fold the back flap of the top layer inside the model.

11 Fold the back flap of the bottom layer inside the pocket you have just created. Finally, spread the bottom layers to make your yacht stand upright.

van

This model uses the same basic technique as the train set. With some experimentation, you can create a fleet of cars of your own design.

1 Crease the center line vertically. Fold the paper horizontally, but do not crease. Make a small pinch at the center.

2 Fold the bottom edge to meet this pinch at the center.

3 Fold down the corners of this bottom flap. Note that the folds do not go all the way into the corners.

4 Blunt these bottom corners by folding the very tips up. Turn the model over.

5 Fold the top edge down so that it lines up with the flaps at the rear. Mountain-fold one of the top corners to the rear to complete your van.

french automobile

This is another variation on the previous models. It captures the distinctive appearance of the classic French 2CV automobile.

1 Crease the center line vertically. Fold the paper horizontally, but do not crease. Make a small pinch at the center.

2 Fold the bottom edge so that it meets this pinch at the center.

3 Fold the corners of this bottom flap down. Note that the folds do not go all the way into the corners.

4 Blunt these bottom corners by folding the very tips up. Fold the top down so that the edge touches the center.

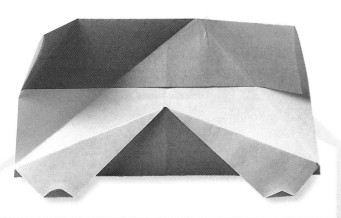

5 Fold down the top left-hand corner. Then fold in the right-hand corner. Finally, fold in the new left-hand edge.

6 Blunt the top corner to complete the shape, then turn over.

chinese junk ....

A traditional fishing boat. As with the sampan, this model involves complex folds. The final pulling step will have to be done gently to avoid tearing the paper.

1 With the white side up, blintz your paper.

2 Fold the top and bottom edges to the center.

3 Now fold the left- and right-hand ends into the center.

4 Fold the four inner corners to the outer edges and return. Now pull out the inside points.

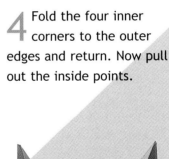

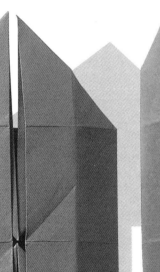

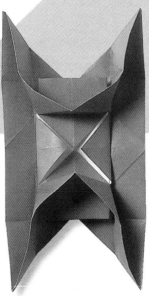

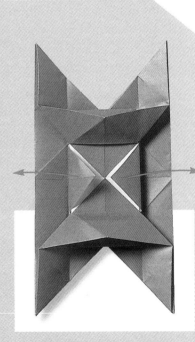

5 Mountain-fold the sides behind to the center.

6 Now open up and spread the top layer.

7 Make squash folds at the top and bottom.

8 Carefully pull out the blintzed corner from the center at the sides.

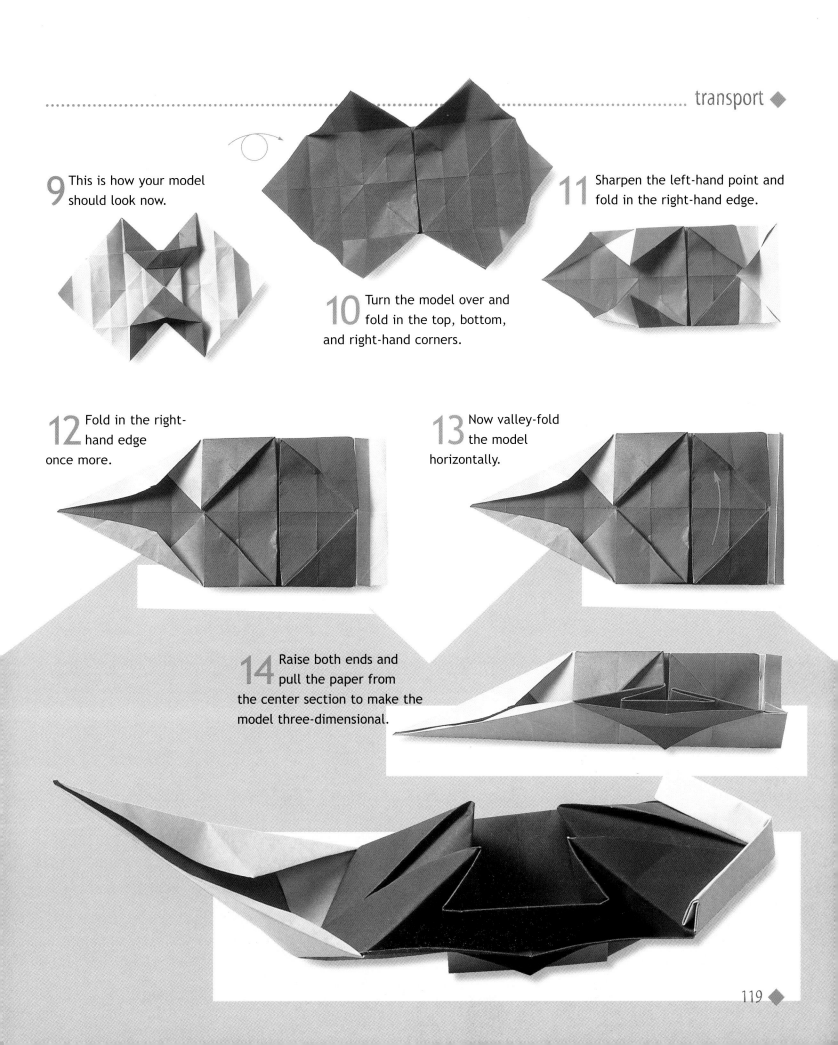

9 This is how your model should look now.

10 Turn the model over and fold in the top, bottom, and right-hand corners.

11 Sharpen the left-hand point and fold in the right-hand edge.

12 Fold in the right-hand edge once more.

13 Now valley-fold the model horizontally.

14 Raise both ends and pull the paper from the center section to make the model three-dimensional.

sampan

This is a traditional Japanese boat. The model has some complex folds and needs to be pulled into three dimensions. You should use thin, strong paper.

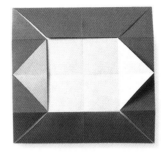

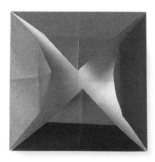

1 With the white side up, blintz your paper.

2 Fold all four corners to the outside edge. Two opposite corners lie inside the other two outside.

3 Mountain-fold the top and bottom edges.

4 This is the shape you should end up with.

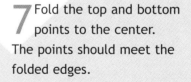

5 Turn the model over and fold the corners to the center line.

6 Fold all four edges to the center line.

7 Fold the top and bottom points to the center. The points should meet the folded edges.

8 Pull from the inside to turn the model inside out. This can be tricky, so pull gently to avoid tearing.

8 complex models

The following projects include creating a three-dimensional model by using a series of narrow folds. Maintaining the accuracy of the folds requires plenty of practice and patience, so these models deserve their own chapter!

vase

Although this model is not too difficult itself, maintaining fold accuracy makes it tricky to complete successfully. Use different-sized paper to create larger or smaller models.

1 With the colored side face up, crease the paper horizontally, but do not fold – pinch at the center only.

2 Crease the bottom edge to the pinch and return.

3 Mountain-fold a new crease to meet the first crease and return.

4 Now crease and return the horizontal center lines.

5 Mountain-fold a crease at the top. The strip should be the same size as at the bottom.

6 Now pleat vertically into sixteenths. Take the time to keep all of the strips even.

7 Now fold up the bottom edge. Then reverse-fold the three bottom strips.

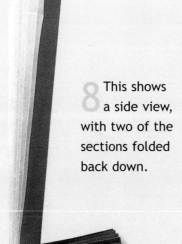

8 This shows a side view, with two of the sections folded back down.

9 Bring both sides together to form a column..

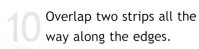

10 Overlap two strips all the way along the edges.

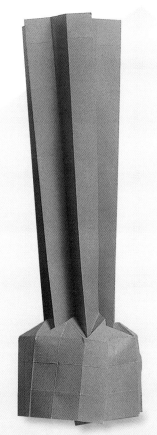

11 Now fold in one section at the top and one at the bottom to complete.

pine cone

This is one of the most complex models to create as it requires precision and patience to make the many small folds. You will need to begin with the colored side of the paper face up.

1 Precrease the square into sixteenths and pleat in the center.

2 Make alternate valley and mountain folds to form a tube.

3 Interlock the flaps. Overlap two of the sixteenths at each end.

4 This shows the tube completely joined.

5 Reverse out all of the side flaps (28 in all). It is best to do one section at a time, unfolding each section to gain access to further sections.

6 This shows half of the flaps pulled out.

7 This shows all of the flaps pulled out.

8 At the top, fold down the tips to lock.

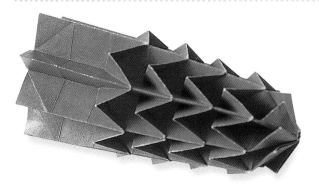

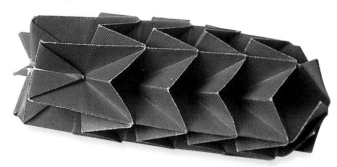

9 Next inside reverse-fold all of the bottom corners.

10 Fold up all seven triangular bottom flaps.

11 This shows all of the bottom flaps folded. Now shape the sides by stretching them.

cactus in a pot

An even more complex design than the pine cone! It requires a 2 x 1 rectangle, and you will need to start with the colored side face up. Use a large size of paper.

Inside view

1 Precrease the rectangle, folding the top half into sixteenths and the bottom half into quarters x eighths. Pleat the top section and make diagonal creases in the two rows above the final row of the top section.

2 Mountain-fold the bottom edge behind. Then valley-fold this folded edge to the central crease. The fold that you have just made should bisect the row. Pleat the top section.

3 Bring the sides together. Form waterbomb bases using the diagonal creases created at the end of step 1.

4 Now join the two edges together carefully.

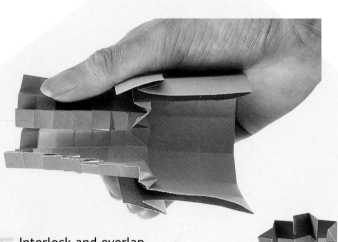

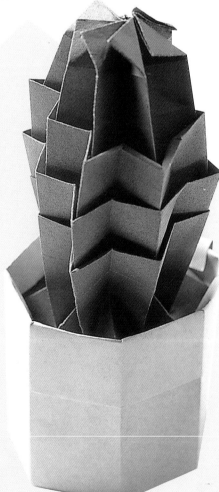

5 Interlock and overlap two of the sixteenths all the way down the join (it is possible!)

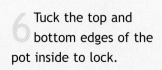

6 Tuck the top and bottom edges of the pot inside to lock.

7 Turn the top corners over to lock. Then stretch each top flap to shape the cactus.

index

where to find out more

If you have enjoyed this book, perhaps you may want to contact other paper-folders. Below are the addresses of some societies. These societies publish magazines and other origami material. They also hold annual origami conventions.

British Origami Society
Membership Secretary
2a The Chestnuts
Countesthorpe
Leicester
LE8 5TL
UK
website www.britishorigami.org.uk

Origami U.S.A.
15 West 77th Street
New York
NY 10024-5192
U.S.A.
website www.origami-usa.org

Some Internet starting points that are useful for new folding material:

David Petty's website
www.members.aol.com/ukpetd

Joseph Wu's website
www.origami.vancouver.bc.ca

Garden of Origami website
www.ccwf.utexas.edu/~vbeatty/origami/folding

credits & acknowledgements

Lilian Petty.

Nick Robinson.

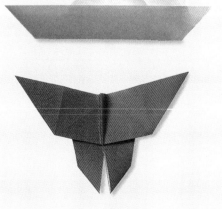

Solution to puzzle on page 69.

5